0055991

DATE DUE

FEB 0 5 1992	
DEC 1 8 1992	
FEB 2 4 1993	
APR. 2 6 1993	
JUL. 7 1993	
JAN. 0 7 1994	
OCT. 1 1 1994	
FEB 2 2 1995	
OCT 1 8 1995	
MAR 2 7 1997	
MAY 0 9 1997	
JUN 1 3 1997	
DEC 0 8 1997	

BABY TALK

The Art of Communicating
with Infants and Toddlers

If you touch me soft and gentle
If you look at me and smile
If you talk to me and listen
I will grow, really grow.
                    – *Anonymous child*

BABY TALK
The Art of Communicating with Infants and Toddlers

Monica Devine, M.A., C.C.C.

Eagle River, Alaska

With a Foreword by
Patricia J. Olmstead, M.C.S.D., C.C.C.

INSIGHT BOOKS
Plenum Press • New York and London

Library of Congress Cataloging-in-Publication Data

Devine, Monica.
    Baby talk : the art of communicating with infants and toddlers /
  Monica Devine ; with a foreword by Patricia J. Olmstead.
        p.   cm. -- (An Insight book)
    Includes bibliographical references and index.
    ISBN 0-306-43762-7
    1. Interpersonal communication in infants. 2. Interpersonal
  communication in children. 3. Infants--Language. 4. Children-
  -Language. 5. Child rearing.   I. Title. II. Series.
  BF720.C65D48 1991
  155.42'236--dc20   90-28793
                                                              CIP

ISBN 0-306-43762-7

© 1991 Plenum Press, New York
A Division of Plenum Publishing Corporation
233 Spring Street, New York, N.Y. 10013

An Insight Book

Printed in the United States of America

"All children are born to grow, to develop, to live, to love, and to articulate their needs and feelings."

— *Alice Miller*

Foreword

Research about what we know of children's speech, language, and learning abilities is growing. There is increasing evidence that the quality of family care given to the child in the hours, months, and first years immediately following birth will greatly influence the quality of the child's development. Parents of all children realize that their children's learning to talk or communicate in any manner will influence how well they do in our society.

The process of learning to communicate is fascinating and a process that is constantly being reviewed by parents, caregivers, and university researchers. We have learned over time that play is a natural vehicle in which to foster this process. Research is abundant to support the notion that children are most interested while playing and probably learn the most while doing so.

Children serve as a model for everyone as they exude energy and creativity in their early formative years. During my personal and professional clinical experiences for the past twelve years, parents have conveyed that their most important desire for their child is to have him feel good about himself and know how to communicate.

In this book, Monica Devine has thoughtfully depicted the process of communication growth, learning to interact, and building meaningful relationships during a child's first three years of life. The chapters are designed to provide an overview of information, as well as give specific activities to nurture interactive relationships. Through social interaction, communication abilities are unleashed. Readers will have an awareness of how to equip themselves to encourage and support language growth through indirect teaching.

This is a book that will be appealing to parents, as well as early childhood personnel. The reader will see its usefulness for all interested in promoting social and communication growth during a child's first three years of life. In every chapter, Devine has summarized and condensed a great deal of current information and provided specific suggestions regarding practical, easy, and fun activities. Her knowledge of the subject matter and sense of humor are most apparent.

I have had the opportunity to interact with Monica Devine through the writing of this book, and, from the beginning, I have been struck by two special qualities that she brought to this project. The first is her first-hand knowledge of her subject matter, as she has drawn from her own experience as a private practice speech–language pathologist serving infants and preschoolers with special needs and their families, primarily in the context of their homes. In addition to this direct clinical commitment, she has always been involved in continuing education opportunities, not only in Alaska but throughout the country. I was equally struck by her unwavering enthusiasm for her subject matter—enthusiasm nurtured by both her professional interest and her experience as a parent. I am grateful to her for both the labor and love she has invested in it.

Patricia Olmstead, M.C.S.D., C.C.C.

Eagle River, Alaska

Preface

The idea for this composition of play activities arose, first, from my journey as a parent and, second, from my experience as a speech–language pathologist working with infants and pre-schoolers.

Observing the growth of an infant in the first three years of life is nothing short of astounding. Growth during this period is faster and more pronounced than in any other of life's passages. What peaked my interest the most was that of the developing communication and language skills of babies, and the fact that I, as a parent, could make some very important contributions to support and enhance those skills.

The content of this material is designed to create an awareness of *how* we communicate with our children, and how we may better equip ourselves to encourage and support their language growth in the first three years of life.

Language is the tool we use to communicate with others. We communicate in many ways: through facial expressions, eye gazing, body movements, gestures, talking, writing, even crying. A child learns to communicate on his own in a very natural way, so why bother to help?

Two reasons come to mind. First, in our society, talking effectively with others is a highly valued skill. Beginning in infancy, communication that is respected and fostered lays a foundation for the gradual development of verbal skills. From first words, to phrases, to sentences, children learn to talk well for many different reasons. As verbal skills progress, the child's parent or main caregiver can make major contributions to the process.

Children who have learned to talk well usually have parents who provide good examples and are not expecting the child to talk like an adult or learn everything at once. Parents who let children make mistakes, who value their attempts at communication, and who encircle them with good verbal input will have children who learn to talk well and communicate their desires and ideas effectively.

Second, and more importantly, good communication with our children allows us to build healthy and lasting relationships. Communication is set in motion the moment you begin caring for your child and continues to take shape in the years to come. Parenting your child, how you talk to him, guide him, and teach him, will in part be *who* he is when he reaches adulthood.

As you thoughtfully participate in your child's acquisition of language, you are creating an interactive relationship that will positively affect his feelings of self-worth. The way in which you communicate with your child and the child's feelings about himself are interrelated and dependent upon each other. A child who feels that what he has to say is worthless will subsequently feel worthless himself. Conversely, open and positive communication with your child transmits to him in a subtle way that his feelings and ideas are significant.

More important than what we do is *how* we do it. Our job is not to change or interfere with a child's language learning, but to simply observe each stage of development and support and encourage what the child already knows. This comes from taking the attitude that small children are innocent, unfolding people, instilled with rights, and, with our guidance, capable of responsibilities. This subtle recognition causes a shift in our thinking and thus a shift in our way of approaching young children, placing more value on and giving more credit to each child's unique learning pace.

Use of the ideas in this book will sharpen your awareness of how you are communicating and indirectly teaching your small child in everyday routine encounters. With this sharpened awareness, you will begin to use these ideas more frequently with your child, enhancing his language skills and establishing a more trusting, open relationship with him in the years to come. It is hoped that this book will give you playful, yet informative, ideas on ways that you can capitalize on your baby's strengths, while continually renewing an appreciation of his emerging personality.

This book was developed for parents, but it is also a very valuable educational tool for early childhood staff and therapists who work with young children. In a country where nearly 80 percent of its children are raised outside of the home, it is hoped that this book will shed some light on a sometimes overlooked, but qualitative, aspect of day care, that of "touching in," or communicating with, babies.

A Word on Gender

So as not to create a bias toward the male or female gender, the pronouns "he" and "she" are used alternately in the text. Additionally, the word "parent," used throughout, represents any caregiver responsible for a child's care, whether caring is in the home, the school, or the day care center.

Monica Devine

Eagle River, Alaska

Acknowledgments

The author gratefully acknowledges Charlie Johanson and Ronda Stoebner for unlimited access to their resources; Kent Devine for his unwavering confidence; Zachary and Christopher Devine for the privilege of parenting; and all the families and friends who graciously let me into their homes to photograph their babies at play.

Contents

Foreword *by Patricia Olmstead* vii

Preface xi

Chapter One   Introduction: Your Baby and Language
Learning 1

Chapter Two   Born to Learn: Birth–3 Months 7

Chapter Three   Babbling Begins: 4–6 Months 23

Chapter Four   Moving About and Socializing: 7–9
Months 39

Chapter Five   Baby's First Word: 10–12 Months 57

Chapter Six   Jargon Talk: 13–15 Months 77

Chapter Seven   Understanding Language:
16–18 Months 99

Chapter Eight   Growth Spurt: 19–21 Months 119

Chapter Nine   Saying "No!": 22–24 Months 137

Chapter Ten   Listen and Learn: 25–27 Months 157

Chapter Eleven   Expanded Learning: 28–30 Months ... 179

Chapter Twelve   Creating Conversations: 31–33
Months 197

Chapter Thirteen   Problem Solving: 34–36 Months 217

Chapter Fourteen   Parents' Questions 237

Chapter Fifteen   Is My Baby Okay? Spotting Potential
Problems in Your Child's Speech and
Language Development 243

Conclusion 251

Appendix A   Suggested Children's Books 253

Appendix B   Suggested Toys for Children: Birth–
18 Months 257

Appendix C   Suggested Toys for Children: 18
Months–3 Years 259

Bibliography 261

Index 263

CHAPTER ONE

Introduction

Your Baby and Language Learning

One of the most exasperating as well as exciting periods in your journey as a parent occurs over the first three years of your child's life. It is within this period of time that extremely rapid growth in all areas of your baby's development is visible.

Through the senses of seeing, hearing, feeling, tasting, and smelling, the infant explores her environment and reaches out to her parents with a thirst for interaction and nurturance. Newborn babies are immediately ready for social interaction with their parents, and this interaction forms the groundwork for learning the language of their culture.

Babies initiate eye contact, enjoy listening to mother's voice, as well as environmental sounds, and communicate many feelings such as pleasure, anxiety, surprise, and discomfort. It is the parent's task to respond to these ever-changing signals as the exciting process of communication begins.

Language can be described as the entire communication system through which we interact. This system includes crying; using facial expressions, body movements, and gestures; and the ability to express feelings and thoughts through words. The foundation of language lies in the affectionate and trusting pre-verbal relationship established between parent and child. Initially, you respond to your baby's cries by taking care of her immediate needs; she soon learns that crying can be used to communicate and thus her desire to communicate is born. Long before speech is acquired, your baby desires to communicate.

Fortunately today, infants are no longer viewed as "cuddly blobs" in need of constant control and total direction. With their fresh immaturity, babies do learn at an amazingly rapid rate. They quickly learn to distinguish between mother's nipple and a bottle. They differentiate people from objects. They know when to anticipate feeding time. A newborn's response to sights, sounds, and touch indicate her hunger for exciting discoveries in the months to come.

Babies are also much more socially aware than previously thought. Gradually, a baby learns that she is separate from others, and a unique personality begins to emerge. So much of her development in the first six months is influenced by the interactions of an affectionate parent or caregiver. Take advantage of the invitation and get to know your baby right from the start.

Fortunate is the baby whose caregiver has the time to actively play with and simply enjoy her. Take the time to respond to your infant. Touch and stroke her, sing to her, smile, and maintain eye contact with her during your caregiving routines.

Your baby is eager to communicate with you through her facial expressions, body movements, and sound-making. As a parent, once you become aware of the subtleties of your infant's communications, you will discover a baby who, in turn, becomes more responsive to you and more interested in exploring her environment.

Consciously be with baby during your caregiving routines. When dressing her, erase from your mind what you're going to prepare for dinner, or when you will schedule the next dental appointment, and simply concentrate on dressing baby. "Touch in" with her by getting eye contact, talking about her fingers and toes, tickling her, and calling her name. In this warm interactive dialogue with your baby, you are fostering language growth as well as developing a trusting communicative relationship that will continue into adulthood.

The purpose of this book, then, is to provide parents or day care personnel with the kinds of activities and suggestions that will promote language growth and build meaningful relationships. As parents, we "teach" language every day and in every situation, whether it be during a specific quiet-time activity, when we're romping around on the floor with baby, or when simply changing a diaper. But we must do so coming from the heart—with patience and perseverance.

Communicating consciously, listening to your child, and guiding her as she struggles to make herself understood will heighten your sensitivity to the real personhood of your child.

Tips on How to Use These Activities

1. The book is divided into 12 sections delineating three-month age intervals from birth to three years of age. Included in each section are an introduction, developmental milestones, 10 activities that you may use during a specific "playtime" you have set aside for your child, and activities to carry out during the daily routines of dressing, bathing, and feeding baby.

It is most helpful to view this progression of activities as a sequence rather than a timetable to which children should be responding. All babies develop at their own speed, with great variability from child to child. Use your own judgment and pick out activities that your child enjoys, and pay close attention to her interests, disposition, and level of attentiveness.

2. The activities in this book are designed to nurture the total growth of the child. One activity is not specifically targeted to accomplish, for example, a motor milestone (like walking) without attention to the child as an individual with her own capabilities, temperament, and personality.

When playing with a child, one cannot separate language

and communication from the activity itself. While baby is stringing beads, exercising the fine motor skill of manipulating her fingers, the parent may talk to her about the activity, share appreciative glances, hug, praise, and give assistance when needed.

The child's motor, cognitive, and language skills come in one package. As you play games with your baby, you are fostering her overall development through your communicative interactions with her.

Language learning can never be separate from the actions and intentions of your child, whether they be active, like riding a tricycle, or inactive, like watching a movie. In order for your child to make sense of an experience, she must gradually form a representation of it in her mind, and the learning of language allows her to do just that.

3. These activities are not designed specifically for fast learners or slow learners; the activities can work with special-needs children as long as they are adapted to the particular needs of the child.

Be more concerned with the activity itself, rather than the age interval. If your child is 24 months old, start with activities in the 19–21-month age range and pick and choose on the basis of interest. Different babies have different areas of strengths, forging ahead with some skills and keeping a slow, uneven pace with others. Always accept and praise what your baby can do, and be sensitive enough to discontinue an activity when your baby indicates she no longer wants to play.

4. You, the parent, are your child's best teacher. Stimulating your baby is a natural part of caring for her while you are feeding, bathing, dressing, and playing with her on a day-to-day basis. Be very observant of baby's responses, however. Some babies thrive on intense stimulation, while others prefer a more toned-down approach.

5. Maintain a sense of humor. You will sometimes be facing comical situations as your toddler struggles to meet developmental demands from the adult world. A sense of humor helps

to dissipate tension so that spills, upsets, and temper tantrums cause less wear and tear on family members.

Participate in your child's play on her own level. Don't be afraid to occasionally "ham it up" and have a good time by acting silly. Most of us have nearly forgotten this special period in a young child's life. We revert to this time as if strangers, tentative in our willingness to join in, but still wanting to make a favorable impression. Shed those inhibitions as you zigzag along the floor pretending to "be a snake" or play "this little piggy went to the market." You'll find your baby has the capacity to bring out the child in you.

6. Be receptive to early talking efforts. Understand that your child is communicating to you in the best way she knows how—often in ways other than with words. Listen to and talk to her about your immediate world, and model language at any time of the day—while changing a diaper, taking a walk, or riding in the car. Tell stories, read books together, and meet your child's need for nurturing with plenty of warmth and love.

CHAPTER TWO

Born to Learn
Birth–3 Months

From the moment of birth, your new baby is exploring the world through his senses. Through seeing, feeling, tasting, touching, and hearing, your baby is already beginning to learn about his surroundings.

The newborn infant exhibits admirable perceptual abilities. He will blink his eyes when a bright light is presented and track a moving object (such as mother's approaching face) at a short distance. His hearing ability is acute at birth; in fact, studies have proven that babies can hear while still in the womb.

The ability to hear sounds and voices is of chief importance to your baby's language learning. Eventually he will learn to talk through cooing, babbling, and imitating the voices he hears. You may have already noticed your baby is startled by a sudden loud noise, or stops sucking during feeding to listen to a new sound. At two months of age, he loves to listen to people talking and can already distinguish human voices from other sounds. Just as he can pick out mother's face in a crowd, he can also distinguish her voice.

During these first few months, your baby's social responsiveness is laying the foundation for communication and later acquisition of language. Your baby is beginning to internalize information when he sees you. He may coo until you return his glance, and then fuss for you to come to him. He may light up when he sees his bottle, open his mouth, and excitedly wave his hands. You'll probably start to spend more and more of your day simply playing with and enjoying him as he becomes more outwardly responsive and expressive toward you.

Initially, your baby's expressive communication will start with his first cry. When he cries, he communicates automatically and soon learns that his simple cry for assistance brings you running. Interestingly enough, each type of cry has its own specific sound and meaning, and, as a parent, you learn to associate a particular cry with a certain type of behavior. You can tell if baby is hungry, wet, or tired by his special type of crying. The hungry cry may be steady and rhythmic while the painful cry may be loud and wailing. Then there's the fussy cry, a drawn-out whimper that may be saying, "I want attention" or "Something's bothering me." Your baby is not actually thinking in this way; rather, you interpret his cries a certain way and he learns to make those associations.

Early cooing sounds that baby makes in the first few months of life are typically nasal-sounding vowels (as if the sound is coming through the nose), produced in the front of the mouth, and several consonant sounds, produced at the back of the mouth. These sounds occur because the baby's large tongue seems to fill the whole oral cavity. As he rocks his tongue forward and backward (movements that are useful when feeding), he makes sounds at the front and back of the mouth. As baby grows, the tongue acquires more room to move, and with this new agility, a great variety of speech sounds occur.

The continual unfolding of a baby's speech and language skills is very exciting for new parents. Sensitive and loving caregivers will lay the groundwork for this process by being attentive to their infant's signals and responding lovingly to his needs.

Developmental Milestones

Listening and Sound-Making

- Hearing ability is acute
- Is startled by loud noises
- Stops activity to listen to new sounds
- Has special cries that parents interpret to indicate hunger, pain, and displeasure
- Quiets down when held and comforted
- Makes eye contact with parent for up to 30 seconds while being talked to
- Responds to parent's voice (widens eyes, smiles, moves mouth) when talked to face-to-face
- Begins to show anticipation of a familiar routine (becomes excited when bottle is seen)
- Makes cooing sounds, made at the front (ah, eh) and back (g, k) of the mouth, which have changes in pitch or a sing-song rhythm

Motor Skills

- Raises head up when on tummy
- Makes crawling movements with legs when on tummy
- When held in a sitting position, holds head up with bobbing
- Brings hands together, loosely closed, toward the midline of body

Toy Play

- In general, infants like to look at:
  - bold lines and features

- ○ high contrast
- ○ simple designs
- ○ bright primary colors
- ○ human face features (especially the eyes)
- ○ bull's-eye pattern
- Watches mobiles
- Follows movement of a toy from side to side (tracking) when it is moved by an adult
- Can hold a rattle for a minute or two when it is placed in his hand
- Reaches toward a toy
- Hits or bats at a hanging toy

Playtime Activities

Cuddling Baby

Communication during your baby's first few weeks of life can best be enjoyed through physical closeness. Because your baby cycles in and out of sleep most hours of the day, he is not yet ready for too much stimulation. Periods of quiet alertness will be followed by drowsiness as baby learns to adapt to life outside the womb.

Skin-to-skin contact with your baby is a necessary component of early social bonding. An infant requires cuddling and comfort when he is agitated, hungry, and tired. Your soothing touch and massage is one way of showing your love, as well as helping baby feel more comfortable with his body.

Studies have shown that premature babies develop faster in their overall development when touch is included in their daily regimen. Low birthweight babies in intensive care nurseries who are regularly held and cuddled by their parents gained weight faster than preemies who did not receive regular physical contact.

Communicate information and feelings through touch by

Hugs and kisses.

regularly holding baby close to your body and stroking and cuddling him. Not surprisingly, most parents have found the best way to soothe a crying baby is to pick him up and hold him close to the shoulder. This behavior usually causes the baby to become more alert and ready to scan his surroundings.

Through holding, stroking, and skin-to-skin contact, your baby learns to trust his environment and increasingly becomes more responsive to those who care for him.

Wrist Rattles

Attach a wrist rattle to baby's wrist. Baby will learn to connect his eyes with his hands, and will discover that waving his arms results in the tinkling of the bells.

Tie a bell to his booties so that when he kicks his legs the bell will sound. Soon baby will make a connection between his movements and the bells ringing and realize that he is making something happen on his own.

Vocal Play

Encourage baby to engage in vocal play. Vocal play is the way in which babies "play" with sounds, deriving pleasure from hearing themselves coo and repeating their own sounds. Begin by making vowel sounds that are already in your baby's repertoire and are easiest for him to copy; babies cannot imitate "new" sounds until after they are seven months old.

Between the ages of two and three months, your baby may enjoy a game of cooing back and forth with you. Call baby's name, get eye contact, make a vowel sound (ah-ah-ah) in a sing-

"Talk to mama."

song voice, then smile and touch baby. Pause to see if he will make a sound back to you. (Be patient and wait; the average response time for an infant this age is up to 10 seconds!) If he does make a sound, simply repeat it after him and keep the game going back and forth a few times. When you hear baby making cooing sounds, talk back to him as if his coos were real words.

In this game, your baby is already practicing making sounds and learning to imitate your mouth movements. Imitating your baby's sounds encourages him to repeat them over and over again. As he matures and becomes alert for longer periods of time, he will enjoy less crying and more "cooing" time with you.

A Social Butterfly

Your baby's particular interest at this stage of development is people—specifically you, the caregiver. He loves looking at your face more than at pictures or toys. He loves watching the changes in your expressions as you talk to him during feeding, bathing, and diaper changing.

Your baby's face will tell you a great deal about his likes and dislikes. Studies show that a baby's facial expressions may be inborn and universal around the world. Your baby's face can tell you how he feels—when he's disgusted, distressed, or feeling pretty good.

Encourage social activity with your baby. Blow kisses, make smacking lip sounds, click your tongue, and vary your facial expressions as you talk to him. In these interactions, your baby is learning early social communicative behaviors such as mutual gazing and taking turns.

Call his name whenever you approach him. Although he does not yet recognize his name, he is learning to respond to the sound of your voice. Using his name frequently lets him know that you are near, and he soon associates your voice with security and comfort.

Touch and Texture

Eventually your baby learns through his senses that he is separate from the external world. He begins to differentiate himself by kicking the boundaries of his crib, batting a hanging mobile, and scooting himself across the carpet on his tummy. He becomes aware of different types of touch—the soothing feel of mother's breath on his cheek, the silky feel of the edges of his baby blanket, and the cool, prickly feeling of water on his skin at bathtime.

Introduce your baby to various textures and fabrics. Dab a cotton ball on his cheek; let him feel a piece of silk slide off his arm; give him the experience of cool grass on the bottoms of his feet. Many mothers recommend the use of lambswool pads in place of cotton sheets in baby's crib. Lambswool provides softness and texture, as well as warmth when it's cold and coolness when it's hot.

Infant Mobiles

At two months, babies begin to distinguish colors from white. You can help heighten your baby's visual development by hanging a colorful mobile over his crib. Start by hanging it on one side of the crib for a few weeks, then change it to the other side. After a couple of months, hang a mobile on each side of the crib to encourage baby to shift his gaze from one toy to the other.

Pick a mobile with two or more contrasting colors and complex shapes. Babies are fascinated by this visual display. During your everyday activities with baby, hold objects up for him to see and talk to him as you walk about his room, encouraging him to follow you with his eyes.

So much to see.

Exploring Faces

Your baby spends hours of time contentedly looking around at his surroundings. Studies show that infants prefer looking at people's faces more than anything else. It's no wonder that an infant's focal distance is about 7 to 12 inches—just enough to gaze at mother while she holds and feeds him. At first, your baby will notice the boundaries of your face, like your chin and hairline. Later he tunes into your features, especially your eyes. Eye contact is a very important element of communication that you share with your baby from the first few months.

To explore faces, lay your baby on his back on the floor and kneel above him, taking his hands into yours. Lower your face close to his and slowly guide his hand to your facial features, naming them as you touch each one. Pat baby's hand on your nose and say "nose"; pat baby's hand on your mouth and say "mouth." Change your facial expressions from time to time, widening your eyes and smiling, or puckering your lips and making kissing sounds.

This type of playful, warm interaction with your baby ensures that he will look forward to your communication time and time again.

Grasping Toys

During the first few months of life, your baby begins to show emerging signs of independence as he learns to grab toys and bring them toward himself for study and exploration. Because of the trust and bonding that baby has established with you, he now has the confidence and security to reach out and discover, an important step in his intellectual development.

Stroke your baby's palm with your finger and notice how immediately he grabs the finger and then lets go. During feeding, he may hold onto your finger for longer periods. Soon his preoccupation with sucking becomes distracted by the actions of his hands.

Give your baby experiences with different objects to grasp. Stroke his palms with wooden blocks, metal spoons, and soft scraps of cloth. Observe his reactions. Does he prefer one over another, grabbing at one toy and not another? Does he watch his hands when they're in front of his face? Eventually he will grab toys and rotate them in front of his face, coordinating his eyes and hands in an effort to understand the world around him.

Baby's Cries

Crying is your baby's way of communicating to you how he is feeling, whether he is hungry, wet, in pain, fatigued, or bored. With maturation, a baby's cries become rhythmical and differentiated so that the caregiver quickly learns the multiple meanings that baby is expressing.

You may respond to your baby's cries in a variety of ways, depending on what you feel are his immediate needs. Some babies may cry for no reason but to simply regulate their systems (as in reacting to the sudden change of being placed in a tub of water at bathtime). Give your baby lots of attention and cuddling, even when he is not crying. Don't worry about spoiling him by responding quickly to his cries. He is setting the stage for communication with you in the best way he knows how.

Ways to soothe your baby (after ruling out a wet diaper, hunger, or a difficult bowel movement) include talking softly and rocking him, walking briskly while holding him at your shoulder or carrying him in a sling, singing, changing his position, and gently massaging his back or tummy.

Prance and Dance

Hold your baby firmly against your chest either in a cradle position or with his head at your shoulder, giving him support at the head if necessary. (When baby is held at your shoulder, he practices head control and strengthens the muscles in his neck as he lifts his head to look around.)

Play soft, rhythmical music and dance around the room, turning and dipping to give baby a varied sense of movement. Hum or sing with the music, watching baby's facial expressions for signs of pleasure or distress which will help you to gauge your movements.

Dancing with Mom.

Activities in Your Daily Routines of Dressing, Feeding, and Bathing Your Baby

Stroke Me Gently

Before dressing baby, give him a gentle massage. Softly stroke the area from his thighs up to his chest, then hold one hand firmly and softly stroke from his wrist up to his shoulder, on both sides of each arm. Conclude by gently stroking baby's forehead and cheeks. A gentle massage is relaxing and enjoyable for an infant. Experiment with light versus more intense touching to see which one your baby likes best. Experiment with various activities during bathing: rub baby's back vigorously with a washcloth; gently splash water on his tummy and legs;

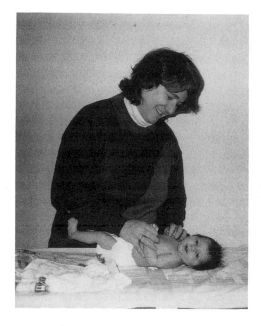

A gentle massage before dressing.

and stroke his arms and legs with a wet washcloth. Also talk to him as you are massaging, softly saying, "Quiet baby, this feels good, quiet baby." Say baby's name frequently and encourage eye contact as you talk.

Rock-a-Bye Baby

Whether breast-feeding or bottle-feeding, make feeding time a positive experience for both of you. Seat yourself in a rocking chair and hum a song while you are feeding baby. Be sure to call his name, make eye contact, and smile at him frequently.

After feeding, rub baby's back in a circular motion when you are burping him. The simultaneous gentle rubbing of his back and humming sounds provide very pleasurable sensations that will eventually lull him to sleep.

Bottle propping in the early months of life is not recommended. In addition to baby's nutritional demands, feeding time provides tremendous emotional warmth that your baby would miss if simply left with a propped bottle to feed alone. Take advantage of feeding times to develop a closer relationship with your baby.

Water Feels Good

Fill the bathtub with warm water approximately one-inch deep. Lay baby on his back in the water on top of a towel, so that he will not slip back and forth on the bottom of the tub, and prop his head up with a folded towel. Place one hand under his head, and with your free hand pour water onto his tummy and legs. If he enjoys the water, he will most likely kick, smile, and wave his arms.

Talk to him while you are doing this, saying, "Oooh, warm water; warm water feels good," and describing your actions.

Follow the Ring

Provide an item of interest near the diapering area so that baby not only pays attention to you but also can be intrigued by a colorful, moving object. Tie a stacking ring to a colored ribbon and hang it over the changing table. During diapering, swing the ribbon gently so that baby will try to follow it back and forth with his eyes.

Describe the movements of the ring: "Look, Justin. See the ring. It goes back and forth. Mommy will push it again. There it

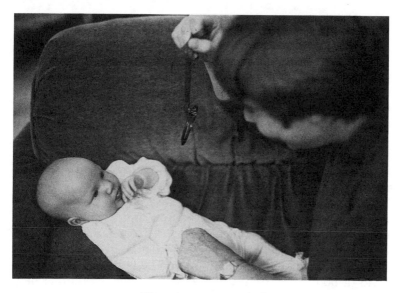

This takes concentration!

goes!" Watching a colorful object swing back and forth encourages baby to move his head and body in different directions to see it. Swinging a toy is also a good distraction for the fussy baby who anticipates the diaper changing process and decides to protest. He may forget about being changed and, instead, choose to focus on the toy.

Some mothers worry about wearing long necklaces that baby may grasp and explore during diapering. Most babies are fascinated by jewelry and find it interesting to tinker with while being changed or fed a bottle. When with baby, wear large wooden beads or string empty spools together on a piece of elastic. Also braid lengths of colorful cord together and to this attach small items (for example, bells, swatches of material, fur). Or simply wear a few shiny chain lengths (baby-proofed) that will be of interest to baby.

Stimulation Techniques

As you can see, stimulating your baby is a natural part of caring for him. The word "stimulation" refers to all the natural things you may do with baby as you respond to his efforts to communicate. Looking into his eyes, holding him, talking and singing to him, showing him toys, and playing with him—are very much a part of his language growth and overall development.

Tune in to your child's sensitivity for stimulation by observing him when you interact. There is no one right way to stimulate your baby. Each child has his own individual needs and moods, and, through your observations and intuition, you will quickly learn just how much play, sleep, food, and activity he needs. When he is alert and "talking" to you, he may seem to be saying, "Let's play some more." When he is fussy and turns his head or body away from you, he may be telling you that he is hungry or tired. In any case, meaningful communication between you and your baby has already begun.

Your baby loves to look at you and listen as you talk to him. During the early months, he will spend most of his time lying flat on his tummy or back. Therefore, at different times during the day, place him in an infant (car) seat so that he can observe what is going on around him and have a better opportunity to socialize with members of your family. You and other family members are your baby's favorite toys!

CHAPTER THREE

Babbling Begins
4–6 Months

The process of learning to talk begins early in life. During her first three months, your baby produced cooing sounds at the back of the throat. With maturation, control of the tongue, lips, and jaw becomes more specific, and the range of sounds your baby can produce increases. The way in which your baby loosely connects vowels and consonants together in strings of sounds is called "babbling." A typical babbled sound sequence may sound like "bababababa" or "dadadada." Now baby has more vocal control, moves her entire jaw when making sounds, and, with the emergence of independent tongue movements, can generate a greater variety of sounds.

Vocal play also becomes much more pronounced. Because your baby is so pleased with listening to herself chatter, she will practice strings of syllables and sound with or without the advantage of you as an audience! Babbling may be called the universal language of infancy. Up to the age of about six months, babies of all cultures around the world babble simple sounds that are almost identical.

You may notice that, intuitively, you are using a very special language when you talk to your baby. This special language called "motherese" is used by adults to get and maintain the baby's attention.

When talking to baby, the pitch of your voice goes up and down in a colorful sing-song manner, which helps you to establish eye contact and maintain her attention. You also naturally exaggerate and elongate vowel sounds ("Hi Sweeeeeetie, Hiiii!") and repeat words and phrases ("Look at Daddy, look at Daddy"). Your facial expressions are exaggerated, eyebrows are raised, and with wide-open eyes you capture and keep baby's attention on you. Speaking this way to infants is our way of getting in touch with them, and, by doing so, interactive and meaningful communication takes place.

Most babies find it very stimulating to listen to speech, so don't presume that because baby doesn't understand the meanings of words, you don't need to talk to her. Some babies may immediately respond by babbling back, and others may remain quiet and study the changes in your facial expressions as you talk. Either way, your baby is taking it all in like a sponge!

Developmental Milestones

Listening and Sound-Making

- Stops crying when spoken to
- Consistently turns her attention to the source of a sound
- Laughs out loud and smiles in response to a familiar person
- Responds to your *tone* of voice, as opposed to the actual *meaning* of words (frightened by "angry" voice; smiles in response to "happy" voice)
- Shows interest in people and objects around her
- Hears and plays with noise-making toys
- Shows expectancy of a toy by reaching toward it, breathing faster, and changing facial expressions or vocalizing to show her excitement
- Makes "raspberry" sounds with lips (puts tongue between lips and blows)
- Opens mouth in anticipation of food
- Vocalizes to her image in a mirror
- Engages in "vocal play" (consists of babbling a variety of

sounds with at least one of the lip sounds [p, b, m] in combination with a vowel)
- May repeat one syllable over and over ("ba ba ba") and chain vowel sounds together ("ah ah ah")
- Uses speech sounds to get attention, reject something unpleasant, and show enthusiasm and anticipation of an event

Motor Skills

- Rolls over from tummy onto back
- On tummy, puts weight on forearms
- Holds head up without support
- Looks around to investigate surroundings
- Lifts legs high when on back
- Sits with support from caregiver

Toy Play

- Puts toys in mouth
- Plays with a toy placed in her hand
- Begins to reach for toys that are in sight
- Looks at objects carefully as if inspecting them
- May wave or shake toys, hitting them on the ground or on side of crib
- Likes looking in a mirror
- Enjoys texture balls, soft squeeze balls, disks or keys on a ring, crib gyms, rattles, and teethers

Playtime Activities

Playing with Rattles

Babies learn about objects in their environment through mouthing or grasping, or feeling toys in their hands and mouths.

Brush a rattle against baby's palm and help her grasp it. Then, move her hand in front of her face and gently shake the

Rattles to shake . . . and taste!

rattle so she perceives that shaking it will produce a sound. Take note how she learns to vary the shaking to make the sound loud or soft by regulating her movements. She may vocalize along with her play, excited by the sounds made by the rattle.

Try to pick colorful, durable rattles that will not easily break or splinter when banged or mouthed. Your baby will shake, wave, and mouth toys you give her, so make sure they are non-toxic and unbreakable.

Have a favorite rattle or set of shaker rings available to baby while riding in the car and running errands with you. Some infant seats have handles for easy transport. Hang a shaker ring, set of keys, or other noise-making toy from the handle to keep her occupied.

Fingers and Toes

Your baby is gradually learning that she is separate from the rest of her world. Through development of self-awareness, she learns that her body parts are a part of her, and that she can move and control them at will. Babies are fascinated by their fingers and toes, and touch, grasp, and mouth them in their drive to explore.

To encourage baby's exploration, rub her feet together, bring them to your mouth for a kiss, or massage them with a little hand lotion. Play "This Little Piggy Went to Market" and count aloud each of baby's toes. Dress her in bright red socks that will draw her attention to her feet, or attach bells to her ankles (they sometimes are attached to booties) to provide incentive for her to reach for her feet. (Make certain that noise-makers are securely attached to prevent baby from pulling them off and swallowing them.)

Apply the same types of activities to baby's hands, drawing them together close to your face (so baby can watch your expressions as you play) and counting her fingers or clapping her hands together.

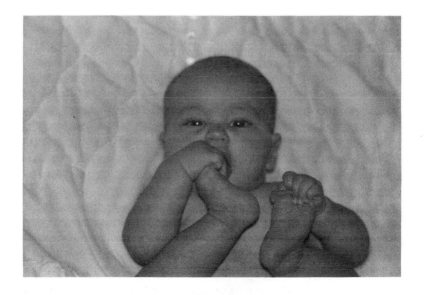

Toes taste good!

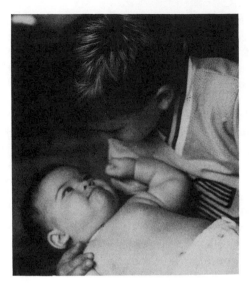

Taking turns "talking."

Let's Take Turns

Choose a time during the day when baby is rested and happy. Cuddle her in your arms and encourage eye contact by calling her name and smiling. When she smiles back at you, say "da da" in a sing-song fashion. When she says "da" back to you, immediately say it again. Babies will often stop vocalizing when they hear your voice so they can listen to you. Pause long enough for your baby to make a sound, then imitate her sound again.

Attempt to take a few turns at this game of sound making, then change your response. Instead of saying the sound back to her, tickle her tummy or kiss her nose. She'll probably enjoy this interaction with you better than any toy you could give her! Don't be discouraged if baby does not babble sounds back to you; she may be "answering" you in other ways (mouthing sounds, waving, smiling).

A very basic element of mother–child interactions is taking

turns. One study showed that mothers begin to teach turn-taking in their newborns during breast-feeding. The baby sucks for a while, then stops. During the pause, mother jiggles or rocks the baby, which is then followed by a burst of sucks. Soon the two coordinate the dance and mother and baby are reading each other's messages—taking turns!

A caregiver helps to shape these social interactions with her baby merely by treating the baby as if she were already an active participant in the dialogue. For example, when talking to your baby, does your conversation often sound like this? [During feeding] "Hiii Sarah. Are you done? OK [removes bottle]. Yumm, that was good." You ask her a question, pause, and watch her face, then answer the question. In essence, mother "puts words into the baby's mouth" long before baby is able to actively participate. With this type of interaction, baby gradually learns that all communication involves taking turns.

Your baby listens attentively when you speak, then takes her turn by "replying" with an excited facial expression, vocalization, or widening of the eyes. Attentive parents naturally take advantage of these moments to socialize with their babies and create "conversations."

Baby's Turn to Lead

After you have practiced taking turns for awhile and taking the lead in the dialogue, give your baby a chance to be the leader.

Lie her on her back on the floor and sit close by her, though with your attention deliberately elsewhere. See if she will try to gain your attention with a squeal, speech sound, or hand wave. Once she gets your attention, respond to her by repeating her action or sound and waiting patiently for her to react once again. Each time you imitate her, she learns that she can "ask" for your response with a gesture or sound.

This is a particularly fun and interesting game, though you need to be observant. Pretending to look away and observing how baby gets your attention will show you just how sophisticated she is in her ability to communicate with you.

Note: Do not be too concerned if baby does not imitate sounds often (if you are confident her hearing acuity is intact). Some babies will put on a good show while others prefer to watch your face and listen. These are differences in the baby's temperament or personality style.

The flamboyant baby thrives on her parent's gregarious style of interacting. The quiet, easy-going baby may withdraw her attention in the face of all the excitement. It takes time to recognize and understand your baby's cues. Although she isn't quite aware of this yet, you know that she is a separate person whose personality and communication style may not mirror yours. As she grows and nature takes its course, her style of interacting will become easier for you to "read" and enjoy.

Mirror Play

Securely prop a Plexiglass mirror up against the couch and lay baby down in front of it on her tummy. This encourages her to lift her head and observe her actions and facial expressions. Give her time to experience this without any interruption from you.

Later, change baby's position to that of sitting. While holding her upright, put your cheek next to hers and play "kiss the baby" as you move your head forward to the mirror and kiss her image. She may reach out and touch her reflection, or imitate your head movements toward the mirror. She may observe the image of her hand in the mirror, comparing it with the real thing. Looking at the changing images in a mirror enhances baby's perception of herself, and adds a new consciousness to her body movements.

As a variation, lay baby on top of the mirror in a crawl position and observe her reactions to herself. Or attach an unbreakable baby mirror to the bumper pad in baby's crib so she can watch her movements and expressions after waking up

"Who's that in the mirror?"

from a nap. Try to discover other opportunities where baby can observe her reflection, such as in glass windows, tin pie pans, and water.

Body Rub

Using lotion warmed in your hands, give baby a full body rub, gently circling the tummy and using slow downward strokes on the arms and legs. Baby will learn to associate your touch with pleasant experiences, especially if you talk softly to her as you rub.

Holding, touching, and firmly rubbing baby's body releases any body tension and establishes close contact between the two of you. Rub the bottoms of her feet, between her fingers and toes, and lightly around her face and forehead. Tell baby what you are doing as you rub, describing your actions in a soft, soothing voice: "Sarah feels soft; soft and silky. It feels good. Round and around Sarah's tummy. Up and down Sarah's legs."

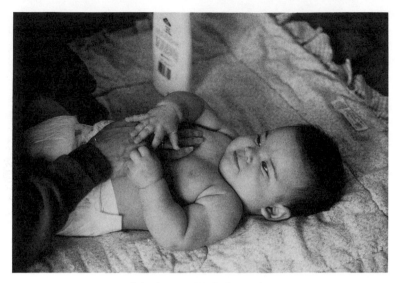

A body massage feels good.

Eliciting Smiles

Parents are naturally delighted with their baby's first smiles. In the first few weeks of life, a baby moves her mouth and lips as if smiling, and she does so without attending to anything in particular. These smiles look almost reflexive in nature, and most parents chalk them up to gas pains.

The genuine smile, with an affective emotional tone, occurs several weeks later. At this time, the baby smiles in response to the caregiver's soothing voice. Later, she pays more attention to facial expressions, and full-blown smiles are more frequently observed.

During your interactions with baby, you can get baby to smile as a reaction to your behavior. Encourage baby to smile back at you by talking to her in an animated voice and making exaggerated facial expressions. Then pause and wait a few moments for her to process the information. Wait for her to respond, either by smiling, waving, or making a sound. Then take your turn by talking and smiling back at her.

To elicit smiles, try kissing baby's tummy or playing a game of "Gotcha." Anticipatory games, such as "Gotcha" or "Peek-a-Boo," elicit smiles as baby looks forward to the surprise and change in your vocal quality. Your baby then learns to associate positive feelings with a happy facial expression. Later, when she sees your happy facial expression, she may kick her legs and anticipate with excitement your interactions with her.

Bicycle Kicks

With baby lying on her back, hold her feet, one in each hand, and exercise her legs by moving them alternately as in riding a bicycle. These movements are prerequisite to her eventual movements of crawling, creeping, and walking. If desired, securely attach bells to her ankles to add extra excitement to her kicks. As you gently move her legs, sing a simple song and establish a rhythm of singing and kicking. Avoid sudden jerky movements.

As a follow-up activity, attach a mobile, noise-making toy, or ball hanging from a string in the area over baby's feet (when she is in her crib or playpen). Adjust the height so that a kick will set the toy into motion. First, swing the toy back and forth and observe baby's reactions. If she doesn't try to kick, guide her leg and foot to kick the toy (but never use force). Accompany your actions with words: "Kick the ball, Sarah. Kick the ball!"

Up We Go!

In the development of self-awareness, your baby feels the stretching and flexing of her body and how her body moves in space as she explores the environment. You can help strengthen muscles and provide physical exercise playing "Up We Go."

With baby lying on her back, wrap her fingers around your thumbs and slowly pull her up several inches toward you. She should keep her head upright and in line with her body, using the neck muscles to stabilize. If her head drops behind, gently guide her back to the floor. Once she obtains good head control, she will be able to follow your lead and eventually rise up to a sitting position.

Talk to her as you are lifting her: "Up, up. Up we go, Sarah." Pay attention to her reactions and facial expressions which will tell you when she's had enough.

Bouncies

Your baby's activity level is beginning to increase as her eye–hand coordination develops and her motor skills expand. On her tummy, she can rock like an airplane with her arms and legs extended and her back arched. She is beginning to move about by rocking and rolling, twisting and turning, rolling from her stomach onto her back, or pushing on her hands and drawing up her knees, getting into a crawling position.

Supporting baby under the arms, play "Bouncies" by gently pulling her to a stand. Slowly bring her up and down, so her feet alternately leave the surface and touch back down. Raise her just high enough so that if she extends her leg, she will feel the hard surface on the bottom of her feet. Say, "Bouncie Sarah, bouncie Sarah, Sarah bounces up and down," in a lively, animated voice. She will enjoy the movement of her body bouncing up and down as she stamps one foot, then the other, as you lift her up and down. Keep your movements light and rhythmic. Quick, jerky movements often frighten babies.

Activities in Your Daily Routines of Dressing, Feeding, and Bathing Your Baby

Pants On!

While baby is flat on her back as you are dressing her, hold her pants up next to your face (so her attention is on you and the article of clothing) and say, "Look, Sarah. See pants." Then

Time for dressing.

move the pants slowly from left to right and encourage her to
follow them with her eyes.

She will track the item back and forth with her eyes, and, as
she's doing so, name the article once more: "Pants, Sarah. Time
for dressing." As you are drawing her legs into the pants, sing,
"Pants on, pants on," in an animated voice. Repeat this exercise
with other items of clothing and encourage her to focus on you
during the dressing routine.

Sounds in the Kitchen

Babies during this stage of development enjoy exploring the
sounds that objects make. Thus, to make these sounds, babies
will bang and pound objects and toys on the floor, highchair,
and other surfaces.

Give baby practice in locating and attending to various

sounds you make in the kitchen. Place her in an infant seat and safely set her on a counter or table where she can see everything you are doing. As you are putting away the dishes, make a variety of sounds to capture her attention. Bang a spoon, rattle some silverware, or stir a spoon in a cup. Walk behind baby, make a sound, and observe how she turns and looks toward the source of the sound. She is fascinated by new sounds and will turn her head to seek any new sounds that she hears. *Note:* You can informally assess your baby's hearing ability by observing what she does when you purposely make sounds with objects that are not visible to her.

In infancy, she responded to loud sounds by blinking her eyes, stopping what she was doing (for instance, pulling away from the nipple during feeding), or jerking her body. Now she turns her head to look at you when you talk, or looks toward loud, unexpected noises. If she does not react, she may have a hearing impairment.

If you suspect your baby is hearing impaired, contact your pediatrician and he will refer you to a hearing specialist in your area. Intact hearing acuity is very important to baby's acquisition of speech and language. Part of her learning to speak and understand is dependent upon hearing her own voice and the voices of others. If not attended to early on, she may experience problems with language and learning in the years ahead.

Sing a Bath Song

Sing to your baby as you are bathing her. Make up jingles that go along with the activity you are engaged in. For example, sing the following song to the tune of "Here We Go Round the Mulberry Bush":

> Now it's time to wash your toes
> Wash your toes, wash your toes
> Now it's time to wash your toes
> My dear Sarah.

Sing the same tune substituting the names of other body parts and including baby's name often.

Time to Eat

Between the ages of four to six months, you may choose to begin feeding your baby strained or pureed baby foods. Some mothers predominantly breast-feed their babies and do not start strained foods until several months later. This is a matter of individual preference to be decided by you, your pediatrician, and your baby's needs.

Initially your baby will suck food from the spoon, and invariably much of the food will be pushed back out! Try only a few teaspoons of food at the first sitting, introducing new tastes and textures very gradually during the first few weeks of spoon feeding. In time, you will be able to cue your baby as to when she should open her mouth for the spoon. A generous amount of your time spent feeding involves communicating with your baby, as you watch her cues when to slow down or speed up her intake.

She will show you with her facial expressions and body movements if she enjoys the menu! Never force-feed a baby; she will show you she has had enough by spitting it out, turning her head away, or fussing. Give her plenty of milk in between spoon feedings.

Feeding time is a wonderful time for interaction: "Look, Sarah. Here comes the spoon. Open up! Yummy, that is good. Do you like cereal? Yum, it's warm and good." Give your baby plenty of time to eat and respond to you. Feeding times (at least for babies) should not be rushed.

Stimulation Techniques

During the early months, your baby learned to communicate her needs through crying. Now she is beginning to communicate with you through eye gazing, smiles, gestures, and making speech sounds. It is up to you to be observant of these social behaviors and respond to her so that communication will continue to be a positive process.

One effective way of enhancing her social-communicative behavior is by playing simple, repetitive, and ritualized games. By playing these types of games with your baby, you are teaching her to communicate with you long before she is able to talk. Playing games with babies teaches them to anticipate certain events or words used repetitively in the game.

For example, you may hold up your index finger and say, "I'm gonna beep your nose," as you slowly move your finger toward her nose. Suddenly you gently "beep" her nose and she squeals with pleasure. Later, she may kick her legs, flail her arms, and vocalize in anticipation of the "beep" when she sees you raise your index finger to begin the game again.

She also learns to take turns in the interactions. You "beep" her nose and she bursts out in laughter. As she rewards you with laughter (every parent's delight), you repeat the action. As time goes on, you will find that the games become more elaborate and your baby is the one to initiate the fun.

Perhaps it is a good idea to schedule a specific play time with your baby each day, when she is happily rested and fed. Sometimes it is easy to get so involved with our daily routines of managing a household and working outside of the home that we forget to spend time simply playing with our children. It need not be a long period; 10–15 minutes may be all that baby requires. Your baby is now utilizing her growing sensori-motor skills of moving, hearing, and seeing, and will prefer to spend most of her day contentedly playing by herself and exploring her environment. Thus, your time investment need not be as great as you might think.

CHAPTER FOUR

Moving About and Socializing

7–9 Months

During the next few months, your baby will undergo a rush of new motor skills, enabling him to become mobile and more exploratory of his world. Sitting unsupported, using his hands freely, turning around, and leaning over to pick up toys gives him greater freedom to explore. Above all, in the next few months, he will begin crawling or rocking on his hands and knees, propelling himself forward to get where he wants to go. His eagerness to move about is relentless.

Just as exciting as his newfound locomotion, your baby begins producing a wider variety of sounds with his vocal play, especially when he is alone and undisturbed. Oftentimes, babies make the most sounds when they are alone, as they explore the sights and sounds around them and test out the various vocal parameters for their own enjoyment.

Babbling behaviors during the 7–9 month period undergo a definitive change characterized by a greater variety of sounds and inflections. Now baby will appear more assertive and *sound* like he is giving a command, making a statement, or even asking a question. He also learns to vary the loudness and pitch of his voice, and can purposely shout in an attempt to get your attention.

A baby's babbling changes in another important way at this stage of development. Rather than producing relatively random sounds, baby will tailor his sounds to those of the particular language spoken in the home. Whereas previously the baby cooed and babbled a variety of sounds, now you can tell if he comes from a Chinese, French, or American household!

When baby makes sounds, he feels the movement of his tongue, lips, and jaw and hears the sounds he is producing. Now he knows that different sounds feel differently. His babbling helps him prepare to form actual words as the memory of making particular sounds is being established. Using actual words to express his needs and desires is a few months away.

Once baby is more motor-inclined—crawling to explore new territories, climbing up stairs, and perhaps pulling himself up to a standing position—his babbling behaviors may tend to taper off for awhile. If this is the case, do not be too concerned, given that you are confident his hearing acuity is intact. He is showing signs of growth in motor areas and is becoming very involved in practicing motor skills. Now that he is able to sit unassisted and use his hands more effectively, he may want to concentrate more on reaching for and exploring all the toys and objects around him, rather than practicing new sounds.

His new motor activities will allow him more opportunities to socialize and learn imitatively from other children. This may be a good time to introduce your baby to a child of similar age for playing and socializing.

Although at this stage your baby will pay more attention to his toys than his playmates, communication between babies begins sooner than we think. Day care directors report that babies actually "make friends" or respond specifically to babies with whom they've had the most contact during the first six months of day care. Social contacts will be brief; baby may sit up and take notice of another baby banging a toy, crawl over to her, and imitate the banging. Fleeting glances, smiles, and mutual grasping of toys will predominate the social arena.

Without a doubt, babies love to smile at, watch, and come into close physical contact with each other. Prop a mirror up against the wall at floor level so they can watch themselves and each other. Occasionally they will imitate one another's behaviors such as clapping hands, laughing, and making sounds during play; this will later become more defined when personalized fighting over toys, as well as genuine friendly contacts, will mark their social relationships.

Including older siblings in baby's play is very valuable to his social development. After an especially hectic day, a sibling can be a great relief and resource for an overworked parent. A baby who crawls away from mother upon hearing the word "diaper" may saunter up to his sister with glee as mother chases him to the changing area. Now the chore becomes a game. Minor risks may become evident when older children rough-house near and around baby, rolling on the floor, stepping over him, and playing chase games with baby in the middle of the whirlwind. But most babies adore watching, listening, imitating, and sharing in the antics of older children. Nowhere else can a baby learn so much than in his own home with children of various ages to egg him on. Besides interest in *his* activity, he becomes interested in their activity as he builds relationships and learns how to get along with them, defending his own interests in the process. Unless there is real concern for his safety, try not to interfere.

Developmental Milestones

Understanding and Talking

- Recognizes his name and turns head toward the speaker
- Understands and responds to "no" or "don't touch" when used emphatically by adult
- Recognizes the names of family members and a few familiar words
- Imitates a physical movement such as peek-a-boo or clapping hands

- Copies nonspeech sounds such as clicking tongue or smacking lips
- Is persistent in trying to get a toy that is out of reach
- Tries to imitate the speech sounds of others
- Puts more sounds together in patterns and repeats them (for example, "a-no-da-ba")
- Begins to use "echolalia" (may try to "echo" words said by others, but the words don't yet have any meaning for baby)
- Begins to use gestures to communicate (waves good-bye, or stretches arms up to indicate desire to be picked up)
- Purposely commands attention of adult (may kiss and hug to gain parent's attention)

Motor Skills

- Sits without need for support
- When held in standing position, enjoys bouncing
- Rolls to one side only, or can roll to either side
- Pushes himself up on hands or forearms
- Rocks on hands and knees, propels himself forward, and begins crawling
- From his back, comes to a sitting position without help
- May pull himself to a standing position, holding onto couch or chair
- Enjoys bath play—kicking and splashing

Toy Play

- Transfers toy from one hand to the other (enjoys squeeze and squeak toys)
- With one toy in each hand, bangs two toys together
- Uses both hands when reaching for a toy
- Is persistent in trying to get a toy that is out of reach
- Puts toys in mouth

- Shakes a rattle, bangs on a musical toy, turns a toy around in both hands while inspecting, as if appreciating its spatial characteristics
- Plays with activity boxes and cubes
- Pushes or shoves large toys (for instance, a beach ball)
- Briefly looks at pictures

Playtime Activities

New Speech Sounds

Set baby in his high chair and sit across from him in his direct line of vision so that you are at his eye level. Make a new sound that you have not heard him use before, such as /t/, singing the nonsense sounds, "tah tah tah tah; tah tah tah tah," with rhythm and inflection. Baby will watch your eyes and mouth with eager interest. Wait a few moments to see if he attempts to imitate you.

Initially he may say a familiar sound that he uses often like "ba ba ba ba." Later he may make an approximation of the new sound, like "da da da da," and, eventually, he will be able to produce the new sound on his own.

Bear in mind that babies vary in temperament and not all babies will be equally delighted with the discovery of their vocal apparatus. Some babies delightfully squeal, shout, and babble for the sheer pleasure of making noise, as well as to gain mother's attention. Quieter personalities may exhibit a more subtle tone of voice, with softer sound making and subdued interactions with adults.

Where Did Baby Go?

Put baby on the floor facing you in a sitting position. Place a light kitchen towel over his head and say, "Where's Justin?"

Peek-a-boo under a blanket.

Baby will pull the towel off of his head and squeal with delight. If at first he doesn't, *you* pull the towel off and exclaim, "Where's Justin? There he is!"

Next place the towel over your head and ask, "Where's Mama?" Encourage him to pull the towel off of your head, and when he does, praise him for his efforts saying, "You did it! Here's Mama!"

This activity demonstrates that your baby is learning that he is separate from other people. He comes to understand that he can have an influence on another person by the actions and expressions he makes. When you pull the towel off, he shows delight, and you start the game over again. Baby learns that he and mother can influence each other's behavior through the interplay of reactions and expressions.

A baby also learns that mother is a separate individual, and that when the towel is over mama's head, this does not necessarily mean she is no longer there. He can tolerate a brief separation and with eagerness will anticipate the appearance of mother's face again, as her image is now fixed solidly in his mind. This growing intellectual capacity opens the door for many new and varied mental accomplishments in the months to come.

Copy Cat

Place baby in a sitting position on the floor. Clap your hands together and sing the patty-cake song. When baby imitates your hand clapping, show him how pleased you are, saying, "Good. Justin plays patty-cake!" Repeat the song several more times, taking his hands in yours, clapping them together and exaggerating the movements of rolling the dough and putting it into the oven.

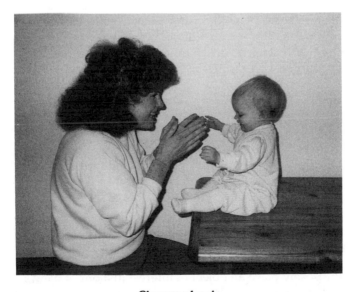

Clap your hands.

After playing this game for several weeks, ask baby, "Justin, play patty-cake?" Does he understand the game before you give him the cues to clap his hands? Does he clap his hands in recognition of the words before you make any movements with your hands?

Play other copycat games in which your baby imitates your motor movements. Ask baby, "How big is Justin?" Then say, "So . . . big" as you stretch your arms up over your head. Repeat this a few times, pausing after your question to see if he will raise his arms. If he doesn't, assist him by placing his arms up over his head. Once he learns the game, he will respond to the question by automatically raising his arms without any assistance from you.

Copycat games are a playful way for mother and baby to develop a relationship and lay the foundation for later interactions through which language is learned. In infancy, children interact with adults on a social level. This social interaction optimizes learning—baby learns to take turns in the game, copies or imitates mother's actions, and refers jointly to objects, toys, or body parts ("Arms up, Justin"). Together, these provide a structure of discourse in which the rules of language are ultimately learned and refined in play with others.

I Want That!

Your baby can balance well while sitting alone steadily for several minutes, using his arms and hands for support when leaning over to pick up toys. Babies between 7 to 9 months old seem to enjoy deliberately dropping objects so as to practice the new skill of picking them up! Your baby wants to explore everything by reaching, grasping, feeling, and tasting; no longer is he happy to simply sit and watch people and things all around him.

Purposely place an object of interest just out of baby's reach and watch his behavior. Reaching out, he may pivot on his tummy to get it. Or he may eagerly crawl, lunge, or scoot on his buttocks in hot pursuit. Each time, move the object a little closer toward you, urging him to follow. Say, "Justin, want the keys? Get the keys. Get the keys, Justin."

Does he become frustrated and turn his attention elsewhere? Does he persevere until the object is happily secured for his exploration? Make it a fun game, not one to purposely frustrate, but one to challenge his exploratory skills and socialize with you in a playful give-and-take.

Little Fingers

Your baby's grasp on objects is becoming more refined; he can use his thumb and first and second fingers to grasp a block and explore it while in a sitting position. He likes to poke his fingers into holes and can successfully pick up a Cheerio or shoelace with his thumb and first finger. This new "pincer grasp" is a major accomplishment, and gives him more dexterity in handling objects.

Give those little fingers opportunities to handle objects of various sizes. While seated in his highchair, let baby play with (and eat) Cheerios, small pieces of graham crackers, and cubes of flavored gelatin (use foods that will easily dissolve with "gumming"). Describe his actions as he practices picking them up: "Justin picked up the Cheerio. Yumm, Cheerios are good. May I have one?" Encourage give-and-take, letting him put a Cheerio in your mouth and taking a few turns at feeding each other. Can he hold onto the Cheerio and look at you at the same time, coordinating his visual attention on you while maintaining fine muscle control? This takes time and practice for little ones.

Commercial toys such as one-inch blocks, pop beads, and balls of various sizes are challenging to hold. Watch baby pick up an old shoestring with a two-finger grasp, which may require a little more persistence.

What's My Name?

Your baby has had a good deal of experience hearing the sound of your voice as you call his name and interact with him during your daily care. A baby's receptive language, or ability to understand the meaning of words, starts at birth with his response to sounds, and, later, his understanding of specific words that are meaningful to him (for instance, bottle and mama).

Encourage baby to respond to his name from a distance. Seat him on the floor and stand about four feet away to his left. Hold a favorite toy or noisemaker that will draw and maintain his attention on you (in addition to smiling at him). Call his name several times and wait for him to turn toward you. Smile and shake the toy when he looks, and give him reinforcement for looking.

Change your position so that you are now behind him, or stand four feet to his right, and repeat the game. Watch how he turns his body or head toward you when his name is called. He is beginning to recognize a few simple words (his name, mama, daddy, bottle) because they are most important to his day-to-day care and are repeated many times throughout a normal day.

Now further increase the distance between you and baby and call his name to get his attention. Call him from the kitchen, bathroom, or bedroom, and encourage him to respond by crawling to you.

Use baby's name frequently in your daily care to attract his attention before feeding or handling. While talking to babies, most mothers automatically tailor their speech to match the baby's understanding. For example, when you speak to baby, do you call yourself "mama?" ("Justin, Mama's here," instead of "I'm here"). Call yourself "mama" in your daily interactions, and baby quickly learns a word for you! Reinforcing the learning of names by occasionally asking baby, "Where's Daddy?" or "Where's Puff?" (the family pet).

Block Banger

When a seven-month-old baby uses his hands, he will pick up one block and put it back down before dealing with another object. By nine months, however, baby may handle two objects simultaneously, with one in each hand. If baby, then, sees something else he desires, he will drop one object and try grasping the new one to satisfy his curiosity.

Provide a set of one-inch blocks for you and baby. With a block in each hand, bang them together repeatedly, saying, "Boom, boom, boom; boom, boom, boom" in a sing-song fashion. Observe how baby picks up the blocks. Does he put one in each hand? Or does he pick up one and try to get the other with his mouth? Hold a block in your hand and present it to him for easy grasping. See if he will imitate your block banging. He may

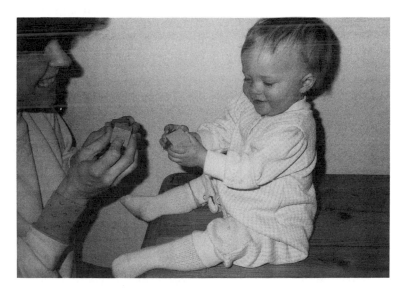

Bang those blocks!

even vocalize along with you, making the /b/ sound or uttering vowel sounds.

Other activities that encourage him to imitate and bring his hands together include hand clapping or banging together toy cymbals or pan lids (if you can stand the noise!). Take turns banging your blocks, saying, "Boom, boom, boom, Justin's turn," and look at him in anticipation. Take only a few turns, then discontinue when baby is ready to move onto something else.

Old McDonald

When baby is well-rested and ready for social play, sit across from him on the floor and play another turn-taking game that will exercise his vocal imitative skills.

Get baby to look at your face, sing *Old McDonald*, sway your body rhythmically, and zero in on his face when you sing "e-i-e-i-o." Stick with two or three animal names for now, singing them once through and varying the quality and volume of your voice to match the animal sounds. Give baby something to anticipate at the end of your song, such as the exaggeration of the final /o/ on "e-i-e-i-o."

Most babies love listening to singing, especially when it is accompanied by exaggerated facial expressions and gestures. Your baby may imitate your rocking and swaying and watch your lips and try to imitate the vowel sounds, or he may do nothing at all but simply absorb your silliness and repeat it at a later time. Babies enjoy and learn from the repetitive nature of simple songs like *Old McDonald, Bingo,* and *The Wheels on the Bus Go Round and Round.*

"Hi" and "Bye-Bye"

Through interactions with their caregivers and siblings, babies learn the various social gestures people use in greetings and leave-taking at a fairly early age.

When you approach baby for a diaper change, wave and say, "Hiiii Justin. Here's Mama." Exaggerating your sounds cues him into your face, which he will watch with interest. When you and baby are in close proximity and he makes a sound that closely approximates "hi" (such as /ah/), say "hi" back to him, modeling the word. When you leave the room, wave and say, "bye-bye." Soon he learns to associate the words with the action. When both of you leave someone's home, lift baby's hand and wave it for him, saying "bye-bye" to your friends.

Later, he may begin to lift his hand or move his fingers back and forth, which shows he understands the ritual. It will take time and practice for him to coordinate verbalizing "bye-bye" with the waving hand movement. At first, he may simply lift his hand and shake it or wiggle his fingers in his lap. Or he may learn the word first, and later pair the gesture with the word. Waving "hi" and "bye-bye" is one of the first meaningful gestures he will use with unfamiliar people outside his immediate family. *Note:* Never force a child to gesture or talk for the purpose of looking cute on your behalf. This will only serve to shut down his future attempts at communicating with others.

Push-Ups

Give your baby encouragement to push himself up with his hands and scoot or crawl to get something. He may be rocking back and forth on all fours, getting ready to crawl. Once he discovers the mobility of crawling, his boundless motivation to explore every room in the house will keep you hopping and unturning every stone to ensure his safety.

Place a pillow or folded towel under him while he is lying on his tummy. Put a colorful, noise-making toy just out of reach and to one side. Shake the toy, set it down, and say, "Come get it, Justin. Come on, crawl over. You can get it!" If he wants it bad enough, he'll lift himself up, reach, lunge, creep, scoot, or crawl. But now you have added an obstacle (pillow or folded towel) for him to crawl over in order to get the toy. Make sure you give him the toy after a few tries. There is no need to frustrate, just encourage his movement and motivation to try.

Activities in Your Daily Routines of Dressing, Feeding, and Bathing Your Baby

Foot Up, Arms Up!

Call baby's attention to the pair of pants you are holding up for him to see. Say, "Let's put your pants on. Foot up please." See if baby is beginning to assist you in dressing by raising his foot in anticipation of his foot going through the hole. If he doesn't raise his foot, you do so and say, "Foot up; put your pants on; foot up."

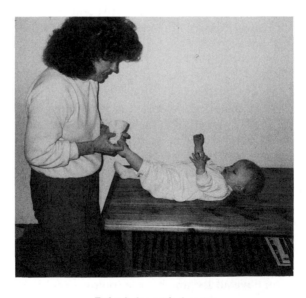

Baby helps with dressing.

Repeat this same procedure when putting on his shirt. Say, "Arms up" and encourage him to raise his arms to assist you in putting on his shirt. By describing your actions in this way, baby is learning the names of his clothing items and body parts, as well as responding to your directions. He is also beginning to become more of an active participant in the dressing process.

Making Choices

Present baby with two different foods and encourage him to make a choice. For example, place a piece of banana and an apple slice just barely out of his reach and ask, "What do you want?" accompanied by your gesture of raising your arms with a questioned look on your face. As he reaches or looks at the desired food, give it to him immediately and simultaneously name the item, saying, "Oh, you want apple."

Also encourage baby to begin pointing to things by taking his hand and placing his pointer (index) finger near the desired item. In doing so, baby not only learns the names of items, but also learns how to use gesture as a way to effectively communicate what he wants. If your baby continually whines to get his needs met, try to gradually shape pointing behaviors using this method, cutting down on the frustration for both of you.

Learning Body Parts

As you play with baby during bathtime, choose two or three body parts that you would like him to be able to recognize when you name them. Play the "get your toes" game. Get his attention and enthusiastically say, "I'm gonna get your toes; here I come, Justin; I'm gonna get your toes," so that he eagerly anticipates your next move. Immediately grab his toes and wriggle them, naming them again. Play with only two or three names at a time, starting with body parts that he can readily see, like his toes and tummy.

As he becomes more familiar with the game, ask him, "Where's Justin's nose?" and assist him in pointing to his nose. At first he may point to a random body part or to *your* nose (because he can't see *his* nose), but after playing the "game" several times, he will begin to get the idea. He may even attempt to say the word after you. Show your excitement over any speech attempt by giving your approval with smiles and a hug.

Cup Drinking

During this stage of development, your baby demands more independence during feeding time. He may grab the spoon (and you can barely pry his hands off) or pat his bottle during feeding, if he is not already holding it by himself.

He is now ready to begin drinking from a cup, with your assistance. First, give him an empty cup so that he can explore and play with it for the sake of becoming familiar with it. Use a small cup and fill it just enough so that you don't have to tilt it too much before baby gets a taste. Go slowly and give him enough time between sips to swallow the liquid. Most importantly, read baby's cues. He will communicate to you whether he wants to continue or has had enough.

The sensation of drinking from a cup is very different from a nipple, and baby will need time to adjust. Initially he may cough a little, bite down on the rim, and lose liquid from the sides of his mouth. With practice (a few sips with each meal), he will learn to coordinate his mouth movements with swallowing and learn just how much milk to take in for each sip.

Show him that you are pleased with his cup drinking efforts: "Gosh, Justin. You're drinking from a cup! It's fun to use a cup, isn't it? Mmmmm . . . milk tastes good."

Later, when he's about 12 months old, your baby will be ready to drink from a cup independently. Provide a small plastic cup, or a Tommee Tippee cup, which has handles on the sides and is weighted to prevent frequent spilling. Using a cup lid will

Learning to use a cup.

help avoid spillage, but try to purchase one with a hole or slit rather than a spout. Spouts encourage sucking, and you are trying to teach baby mature tongue and lip movements charac teristic of true cup drinking.

Stimulation Techniques

Adult communication is a "game" in which each player takes a turn in the interaction. You speak, the listener pauses and listens, and then takes his turn at speaking. In early infancy, you are promoting this communication game with your baby in a social way. Although he is not yet using words, he is beginning to use early social-communicative behaviors in the form of giving, reaching for, and pointing to an object while he is looking at you. Capitalize on these communicative behaviors, as these are the moments in which you are bridging the gap between his early communicative behaviors and his use of real language in the form of his first words which are soon to come!

For example, if your baby sees a toy which is out of reach and then looks at you and begins to fuss and vocalize, you can be sure that his intention is to acquire that toy. As you pick up the toy, name it and ask baby, "You want the ball?" Wait a few seconds for an affirmative response, such as increased breathing and sound making, flailing arms, or an excited facial expression. Then give the toy to him saying, "Here's the ball, Justin. There you go."

Notice the difference in the intonational patterns (the singsong of your speech) of the two phrases, "You want the ball?" and "Here's the ball." Your baby is cueing into those small differences in your speech long before he understands any of the words, and initially derives a great deal of meaning by the rhythm and sound of your voice.

You may have already noticed that he is imitating your singsong in his babbling so that he sounds as though he's asking a question or making a demand. When he's hungry, perhaps he looks to you and then at his bottle, which is out of reach, and uses a demanding tone of voice as if to say, "Feed me." These sounds are very subtle communicative behaviors that most parents are naturally attuned to in reading their baby's signals. It is truly amazing how much and how well babies are able to communicate without the use of real words!

CHAPTER FIVE

Baby's First Word
10–12 Months

Mama—perhaps your baby's first real word. What a memorable milestone! Your baby's first word may occur anywhere between 10 and 14 months. As a parent, it may be hard for you to decide just exactly when she said her first word; after all, she has been communicating with you all along with strings of sounds in a meaningful way. By selectively reinforcing certain sounds baby makes, you can help her discover that words are very powerful tools. You are teaching her the value of language.

For example, when baby utters "mama," mother immediately shows her pleasure by rewarding baby with a kiss and a smile. From this, baby connects that warm familiar person with the word "mama," and soon acquires a real word to depict a very important part of her world. Mother naturally motivates baby to use real words in many situations throughout the day. While looking at books together, baby may point to a picture of a dog and say "da." The picture is a representation of what she sees and acts upon every day, namely, the family pet. When mother responds by saying, "Yes, dog; that's a dog," in a delighted, cheerful manner, baby begins to form a connection in her mind between the picture and the spoken word. She continues pointing to other pictures on the page, waiting for mother to name them for her.

Babies learn words that pertain to the actions and objects experienced in their everyday lives. Most of your child's first words may be nouns, names of objects she manipulates or experiences in her daily routines. She does not simply learn words in a rote way, but actively formulates meanings in her mind so that language learning proceeds from an active experience (like diaper changing) to understanding and saying the word (diaper). When using single words, babies are doing much more than simply naming or imitating. They are using one word to express a complete thought; thus, a single-word "sentence" can mean any number of things depending upon the context in which it is spoken. "Dada" can mean many things when uttered in different situations; it can mean bye-bye as baby waves daddy off to work, or that those keys belong to daddy as baby pulls them out of his coat pocket.

When starting to talk, some children predominantly use nouns, while others use social greetings (hi and bye) to influence another's behavior. So don't worry that your child is not yet calling you "mama." She may be more interested in the family pet, and "Puff" the cat will be graced with the honor of her first real word. Or maybe getting something to eat and drink is a top priority, so that her most frequently used word is "baba" (bottle), "du" (juice), or "kakoo" (cracker).

Of course, this is only part of the story. In learning to talk, your baby must also be motivated to try. If her needs are catered to, or if she has an older sibling who does all the talking for her, she will soon realize she hasn't much need to verbalize her wants.

Children from highly verbal homes have a tendency to talk earlier than those children whose every need is anticipated and catered to. Learn to be aware of those situations in which you can encourage her talking when she is trying to communicate through pointing or whining. Before promptly giving her what she wants, name the item she is pointing to, make a comment about it, and then give it to her. This way she learns that language is useful in expressing her needs and wants.

When your baby starts using real words, try to refrain from excessive praise for every new word acquired. She will understand from the warmth you exude in the conversation that you are proud of her ability to express herself. More important than a word tally is the fact that you respect her attempts at communication and are not judging her performance.

You can turn everyday activities into language learning experiences by talking to your child about the activities and situations she is experiencing throughout the day, at home or in day care.

Developmental Milestones

Understanding and Talking

- Looks toward the source of environmental sounds, such as a noisy vacuum cleaner or a doorbell ringing
- Recognizes new words (usually foods, favorite toys, names of family members, common objects)
- Understands simple commands such as "come here," "sit down," and "don't touch" when used emphatically
- Imitates gestures as in patty-cake and peek-a-boo
- Waves bye-bye
- Shakes head "no" in refusal, and cries or throws tantrums when angry
- Is developing a sense of humor, and repeats an action or sound if adult laughs or claps for her
- Imitates nonspeech sounds such as coughing or tongue-clicking
- Tries to imitate new speech sounds after an adult
- Vocalizes along with music
- Exclamatory speech may consist of "uh oh," "ouch," and "pop!"

- Says first word; may use a few words specifically, such as "mama," "dada," and "bye"
- May use a specific word frequently, then discontinue saying it for several months

Motor Skills

- Crawls over and around things while holding a toy in one hand
- Stands for a few moments without assistance
- May begin taking tentative steps
- Walks sideways while holding onto the couch
- Begins to stoop down and try to pick up a toy
- Can remove a lid from a container
- Throws or flings objects

Toy Play

- Takes toys out of the toybox
- Copies actions such as stirring in a cup
- Finds toy hidden under a box, showing awareness that object exists when out of sight
- Purposely drops an object just to watch it fall
- Enjoys container play—putting objects in and dumping them out
- Pulls a string toy
- Likes to play with household objects or any interesting item within reach, as well as the contents of kitchen cupboards
- Plays "on the run"—explores one object for a few minutes before moving onto the next
- Can stack two blocks
- Looks at pictures in a book and turns a few pages
- Enjoys rolling and throwing balls

• Likes pop beads, roly-poly toys, activity boxes, stacking ring cones, easy pop-up boxes, containers with items to empty and fill

Playtime Activities

Let's Read

Your "reading" time together at this point will consist of looking at books and simply naming and describing their contents for baby. Start out with just a few minutes of "reading" at each sitting, until your child develops a longer attention span.

Choose books that have large, colorful pictures of animals, toys, and other familiar objects that baby will enjoy. Small baby books with hard, stiff pages will wipe clean and are impossible

Listening to mother read.

for her to tear. Picture books without much written text are appropriate. However, if there is text, you need not read the whole story. Make up your own short version or simply point to the pictures and name them.

Set baby on your lap, identify the book by placing your hand on it, and say, "Book. Let's read Sarah's book." Use a calm, yet lively, voice as you point to and name different pictures: "See the doggie. The doggie's eating." Eventually your baby will begin randomly pointing to pictures on the page. When she does so, be sure to stop and name the pictures for her. Let her set the pace by allowing her to turn the pages of the book. She may skip pages, turn them from back to front, and turn the book upside down. This is fine; she is exploring the range of possibilities. Books are not just for reading; they're fun to play with too!

By enjoying books together, you are exposing baby to reading readiness skills, as well as providing a closeness that will make a lasting impression on her attitude toward reading in the future. And you want this early impression to be favorable, as the time children generally spend reading in the elementary years is in tough competition with television viewing.

Go into any children's bookstore and you are faced with hundreds of books to choose from, which can be a bit overwhelming. At this age level, stick with picture books, nursery rhymes, and simple traditional storybooks. It is not necessary to purchase a large quantity of books; local libraries are usually well stocked with childrens' books, and an experienced children's librarian can help you choose books appropriate for babies.

Hats On!

Put several hats into a box and sit facing a mirror with baby seated next to you. Pull a hat out of the box, place it on your head, and say, "Hat on. See my hat? It's on my head. Now it's Sarah's turn. Find a hat!"

Encourage baby to imitate your actions by pulling a hat out of the box and placing it on her head while looking in the mirror and laughing at how silly you look. She may try to imitate your words as well, so try to keep your utterances short and to the point, describing exactly what you are doing.

Social behavior is learned by copying what others do. Your baby learns to wave bye-bye by watching others wave. Eventually she learns to put on her hat and coat, eat with a fork, and ride a tricycle, all by imitating others. Imitation is a natural way of learning, and a new dimension is added when the child sees herself in the mirror copying the adult's action. Try making funny facial expressions for her to copy, to go along with your display of silly hats.

Older children will take hat play a step further. Already familiar with where to place the hat, an older child moves from imitation to pretend play, taking on the role of the person wearing the hat. Most preschools and day-care centers provide dress-up clothes for make-believe play, with hats for specific roles (policeman, fireman, baseball player, chef, etc.).

Uh Oh, Fall Down!

Set baby in her highchair and place one favorite toy on the tray in front of her. Pretend to accidentally knock the toy off the tray and immediately exclaim, "Uh oh, fall down!" with an exaggerated wide-eyed look of surprise on your face. Baby will visually follow the toy to its destination (as she hangs over the tray) and reach out in an attempt to obtain it.

Now pick up the toy and put it back on the tray. Wait and watch if baby will purposely knock it off and imitate your exclamation of "uh oh" as it falls to the floor. (Hopefully she will not generalize this game during mealtime and purposely fling her cereal bowl to the floor!) Play the same game with blocks, building a high tower and knocking it down. Babies usually enjoy imitating highly intoned repetitive sounds such as "uh oh" (toy falls down), "pop pop" (blowing bubbles), and "bye-bye" (wave).

Find the Tinsel

Your baby has graduated from the raking, grasping movements of the six-month-old to a more refined ability of using her fingers and hands. She enjoys handling small objects and can hold items neatly between her thumb and first finger.

Save a few cardboard toilet-paper rolls and use them for interesting seek-and-find games that challenge baby to pull out all the contents and stuff them back in. Stuff a roll with cotton balls, decorative Christmas tinsel (the reflective gold and silver

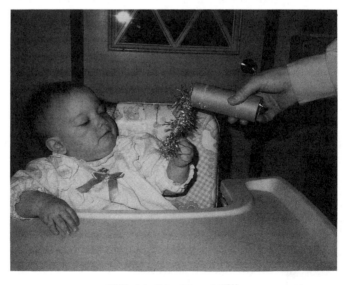

"What is this shiny stuff?"

kind used to drape on trees and walls), the grass used in Easter baskets, or white tissue paper. Inside, near the middle, hide a small toy, such as one of the Fisher-Price people. Encourage baby to pull the stuffing out and find the toy. Prompt her by saying, "Let's pull this out. Can you do it? Pull it out. What's inside? Keep pulling. Oh, *there* it is! A little man!" Initially, give a couple of pulls on the stuffing to demonstrate it for her and then let her explore on her own (which she may do without your help anyway!). Most babies will explore with interest and curiosity, especially if the stuffing has a pleasant texture (cotton) or is illuminating and catches the eye.

Paper Crunch

Why do babies get such a kick out of paper? Did you ever notice how they love diving into your newspaper, or, in the midst

Crunching paper is fascinating.

of a heap of commercial toys, will choose to play with the final draft of your business report? Babies are delighted by the sound of crinkling paper. To keep your important documents safe, while giving baby an opportunity to explore the properties of objects, play "Paper Crunch."

Give baby various kinds of paper to explore. Old grocery bags, waxed paper, white tissue paper, or notebook paper are best. Avoid newspaper or colored tissue paper, as the print and color tends to bleed, and baby will invariably want to enjoy a taste of this fascinating stuff. She will explore the paper by waving, patting, and rumpling, becoming fascinated by the sounds and feel of the paper as it changes shape in her little hands. Supervise her play so that large amounts of paper don't get swallowed!

Mommy Who?

By the time she is twelve months old, your baby has become aware that mother and father are separate individuals from herself. She can easily pick out mother from a roomful of other women, and now associates her familiar face with not only getting her needs met, but simply the pleasure of social approval and play.

Change your looks slightly and observe baby's reactions. Wear a pair of glasses, put a shower cap over your head, or wear a floppy oversized hat. Watch baby's reactions of surprise and, perhaps, puzzlement. Caress and talk to her so that she recognizes you as the person she has come to know and trust. Remove the unusual item and reassure baby by saying, "Look, it's Mommy. She has funny glasses." Make sure you do not frighten baby with anything too overbearing or gawdy. Simply have fun with different props that will pique her interest and be enjoyable for both of you.

Slap Hands

Babies are quite adept at imitating the actions of others as they approach the one-year age level. Initially, babies will imitate familiar movements, or ones that they already do in their play. For example, if you have seen baby bang a spoon on a cup, and she does it again after watching you, she has copied a familiar movement; one that she already does in her play. The ten-month-old is ready to copy unfamiliar movements as well, ones that may not be familiar to her normal play routine.

Observe your baby's ability to immediately remember and carry out a gesture by playing a game of "Slap Hands." With baby in your lap, facing the dining table, playfully slap your hand on the table. She will follow. Then slap a couple of times and watch how she imitates. She is not ready to imitate compli-

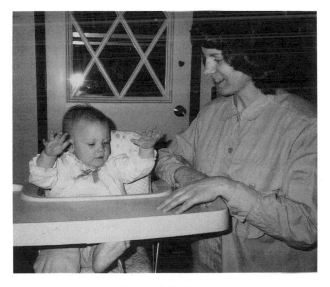

Patting baby's tray.

cated rhythms, but will alternate hands as you do (sitting be-hind baby, she can easily follow your hands). Each time you slap, say, "Boom!" Oftentimes, when pairing a gesture with an inflected word, babies will try imitating the word or initial sound of the word in their play.

Gross motor actions are the most fun and easiest to copy at this time. Simple actions she will enjoy copying include clap-ping hands, spreading her arms out wide, waving, and rolling hands as in "patty-cake." Later on she will be interested in copying a sequence of actions and differentiated finger move-ments when she is ready to participate in finger plays and songs.

Stair Climber

The ten- to twelve-month-old may be starting to walk, but may still prefer to crawl. Of special interest at this time are carpeted stairs, which offer a challenge to explore other spaces, as well as new ways to move the arms and legs. Your baby now experiments with the new sensation of alternately moving both sides of her body on a different plane (going up stairs rather than across a floor).

If your baby is eager to try and you're concerned about falls, you can use a gate. Or you can take the time to show baby how to climb backwards down the stairs, arriving safely at the bottom after an adventurous workout.

At first, your baby will be persistent in climbing forward and may thwart your attempts at any help. Let her explore freely with your supervision. Then move her legs, one at a time, to the next step, and describe the action: "Down we go, Sarah. Let's climb down. Leg down. Other leg down. Good, you're climbing down!" Once she gets the hang of it, she will practice and prac-tice with confidence and delight. (Never leave baby unattended near a lengthy flight of stairs.)

Making that first descent!

Horsey Rides

While you're sitting comfortably in a chair, set baby on your lap, facing you, with her bottom close to your knees. Slowly bob her up and down, and hold her by the hands or under the arms for support. Sing slowly, "This is the way the farmer rides. Giddy-yap, giddy-yap." Next, increase the speed a little, bobbing her a bit higher, and singing, "This is the way the lady rides. Trit trot, trit trot." Finally sing, "This is the way Sarah rides", and bounce her up and down vigorously (just short of the bucking bronco), ending the game with laughter and hugs.

Once baby is familiar with the game, she will be able to anticipate the surprise or high point of the ride, and may later come to you and initiate the game herself by crawling up onto your lap and bouncing. She learns when to tense her body to hold on with better muscle control. Gradually, she can sense the timing of your rhythms, and tells you by her squeals, howls, and facial expressions if you're going too fast or slow for her.

A simple game of horsey rides fosters social communication, bringing laughter and closeness between you and your baby. There are many different "knee games" to play, and sitting a baby on your knee is perfect for lively interactions to take place. You may also hold toys in front of her for her to reach, teasing her a little in your play.

Goodnight Song

The one-year-old engages in intense activity that parallels her rapid physical growth: standing, walking, scooting, rolling. She has enormous energy which may often result in resisting bedtime. Rocking and singing will help to calm a very active baby, but plan on spending up to half an hour lulling her off to sleep. Try not to overstimulate her just before bedtime.

Establish a rhythm by quietly clapping your hands or rubbing baby's back as you sing. Sing a favorite lullaby or make one up as you go along. Use baby's name frequently and use words that are repeated often, such as:

>Goodnight Sarah
>Sarah goodnight
>Goodnight Sarah
>See you in the morning

Sing several rounds of the song, substituting your baby's name with names familiar to her (Daddy, Mama, sister). Your baby will look forward to your bedtime ritual, whether it be to read a book, sing a lullaby, or enjoy a massage. This contact gives her a sense of security and trust that will follow her into childhood.

Activities in Your Daily Routines of Dressing, Feeding, and Bathing Your Baby

Diaper Time

Your baby immediately recognizes when it's time for diapering when she sees you approach her with a diaper in your hand, or when you carry her to the familiar changing area. Because she has been through the routine before and recognizes the cues that make up her understanding of the event, she can anticipate what to expect.

Give her the words to match the diapering experience.

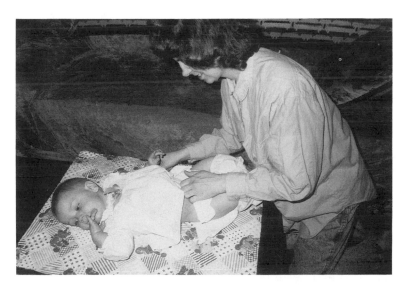

"Not this again!"

While carrying her to the changing area, announce in a lively voice, "Diaper time. Let's go change Sarah's diaper." Gently tug on both sides of the diaper and again describe your actions by saying, "Diaper time; change Sarah's diaper," in a sing-song fashion. Soon she will come to recognize the word "diaper" and know what it means. She then will not need to see a diaper in your hand to know what will happen next. Pairing the label with the activity teaches her a new word, which, when voiced alone, has meaning for her.

Some babies at this age will immediately lie down when mother mentions the word "diaper," in anticipation of being changed. Others will deliberately try to run the other way because they do not enjoy the changing process. Both behaviors indicate that baby understands and can anticipate what comes next in the routine.

More Milk

Give baby a cup with a small amount of milk at mealtime. (Make sure her high chair is pulled up to the table so she is included in the social interaction with the rest of the family.) As you hand her the cup, say, "Here's your milk; mmmm, milk is good." After baby takes a few sips, reward her for good cup-drinking behavior (it will be sloppy at first) by saying, "You did it; that's nice cup-drinking."

When baby is finished, she may outstretch her cup-wielding hand for more. If she gestures to you for "more," immediately say, "More milk? You want more milk?" and then pour some into her cup. By acknowledging her gesture for "more" and verbalizing her desire, you are giving her a good example of how to use words to get what she wants.

At nine months of age, she may have fussed and cried to let you know she wanted more of something. Later, she held out her hand and gestured, making sounds to get your attention. And finally, at around the one-year-plus age level, she can use real words to get what she wants—quite an accomplishment indeed.

Rub-a-Dub-Dub

Music and singing songs are very pleasurable ways to socialize with baby and teach her about language. Most children are naturally inclined to respond to music, feeling the warmth and energy inherent in simple melodies. Later in the preschool years, you can help your child discover the sound of her own voice in song by encouraging her to sing along with you.

Using a wet washcloth and rubbing baby's arms and legs, sing the following:

> Rub-a-dub-dub
> Sarah's in the tub
> Washing, washing
> Rub-a-dub-dub

Sing this repeatedly, using your child's name and showing a number of delightful facial expressions. Baby will enjoy listening to the simple rhymes and words, and may try to join along in the song.

Also, point out various body parts as you wash, and make a rhyming chant as you go along, such as, "Wash Sarah's feet, wash Sarah's nose, wash Sarah's ears, and wiggle her toes."

Finger Foods

Giving your child the opportunity to feed herself allows her to enjoy the sensory properties of food and learn to develop her own eating habits. You can start letting your little one finger-feed as early as nine months. Through trial and error, she will

Finger foods for kids like me.

gain experience using her fingers to pick up small bits of food, as well as coordinating hand-to-mouth movements in finger-feeding.

Provide soft, bite-sized foods at snack time. Let her explore the contrasts between crumbly melba toast and soft, slippery slices of banana. Other good finger foods include bits of scrambled eggs; Cheerios; diced, cooked potatoes; cookies; crackers; peeled, chopped fruits; soft, ground meat; and bits of bread. Give only a few pieces at a time, so that she must ask for more when she is ready. When she wants more, let her tell you, either with words or gestures.

Remember to name the items of food. She will quickly learn the names of food items if you are conscious of naming them for her at each meal. *Note:* The following finger foods should be avoided due to possible choking or hard consistencies: peanuts, popcorn, hard candy, hot dogs, grapes, chips with pointed edges, and any other items that require thorough chewing.

Stimulation Techniques

Perhaps the very essence of your interactions with baby is evidenced in the enthusiasm you communicate to her during these activities. Communication is much more than just talking and listening. Emotions are expressed through body language; tone of voice, posture, facial expressions, distance between each other, eye contact, and touching all reveal facts about ourselves without the use of words. Your nonverbal body language will convey to your baby how much you enjoy her and if you are relaxed, tense, upset, or happy.

You, in turn, can recognize how your child feels at any given moment by reading her body language. A mother can easily interpret many emotions—hunger, pleasure, anger, excitement—all from baby's facial expressions and the tone of her voice.

During your play time together, try to impart your enthusiasm and love of life to your baby through your patterns of speech. Using colorful, inflected speech is much more interesting and fun to listen to than a monotone quality of speech. When talking with baby, remember to use rising and falling intonation on words such as "uh oh," "fall down," "all gone," "thank you," and "bye-bye." The sing-song quality of your voice tells her that you're happy to be with her and also helps her to learn the words without pressure. Before baby imitates the words themselves, she may imitate the melody of the words, which eventually will be shaped to sound like real words.

Try to make use of *onomatopoeia*. When you use onomatopoeia, you are naming an object or action by a vocal imitation of the sound associated with it. One-year-olds adore these silly sounds in your play. Some examples include "rrrrrr" while playing with a toy car; "pop pop" while blowing bubbles; "bbbbbbb" while sailing a boat in a tub of water; "mmmmmm" as you lick an ice cream cone; "bzzzzzz," the sound of a bumblebee; and "shhhhh," the sound of running water. Attaching sounds to your daily activities such as "shhh," as you run baby's bath water, or "pop" when the toast pops up, will delight your child and encourage her to try saying them along with you.

CHAPTER SIX

Jargon Talk

13–15 Months

Has your child ever imitated you scolding another child without using any real words in his strings of sounds? With a toy telephone, does he sometimes sound like he is carrying on a conversation, without words? Does he ever *sound* like he is making a demand or asking a question?

By now, baby has learned to duplicate the theatrical elements of your speech, copying how he has heard you speak to others, and perhaps mirroring your own moods and feelings from time to time. This gibberish is also known as *jargon talk,* when baby sounds like he is talking in phrases or sentences. However, there are very few real words present.

When you hear your child using jargon talk, take advantage of this pretend conversation time. Even though you don't understand any real words in his gibberish, talk back to him as if you really do and comment on whatever you think he would be saying if he were using adult sentences. Your child is learning the fundamentals of conversation in this practice, for instance, changing the pitch of his voice to indicate a change in mood, taking turns talking, and pausing between the different topics of your pretend conversation.

Some children completely skip this jargon phase, especially

those who begin to talk very early. Others use jargon after they've acquired real words, and still others may revert back to jargon periodically. This is not the least bit unusual. Children progress on the same path toward learning to talk, but with many individual variations along the way. Many more real words are yet to come, and jargon usually disappears altogether by 2½ years.

It is important to be patient with your toddler's attempts at speech. His production of speech sounds is very imprecise and immature. Because of his home environment, he will learn English. But, because of his innate capacity to learn language, he is driven to create his own language first. He may say "da" for daddy, "gog" for dog, or "ta" for cat, and, to him, these sound combinations have meaning. At this point, there are no errors. Baby uses personally chosen sounds to represent the people and objects in his life.

One rarely considers just what is involved in learning to talk. The mouth, tongue, and lips utilize dozens of small muscles that must work together in synchrony to produce different speech sounds. It takes months of practice to coordinate these muscles and to get the sounds in the right order to form words. The way you move your tongue, lips, and teeth determine the distinction between different sounds. For example, for /t/, your tongue goes behind your teeth on the roof of your mouth, with an abrupt flow of air; for /sh/, your teeth are clenched together with a forward, prolonged flow of air. In a sense, learning to speak develops naturally. But, it wouldn't happen at all if baby were not able to hear and see others talking, practice the sounds, and respond to other humans.

Although a child does not consciously think of the many movements and muscles that require precise coordination for speech, he learns by feeling his mouth movements and repeating the sounds over and over again. The progressive development of his ability to say different sounds correctly is not automatic; it is a learned behavior, and will take your toddler another year to produce intelligible words that clearly match adult

speech. In the meantime, listening to the gibber-jabber of a fif-
teen-month-old is delightful. With as many as eight real words
in his expressive vocabulary, and the vocal elements required to
carry on pretend conversations, communication continues on its
jagged, yet predictable, path into childhood.

Developmental Milestones

Understanding and Talking

- Tries to imitate gestures and speech sounds of adults
- Recognizes the names of 10 familiar objects
- Understands short and simple sentences that are familiar to
  him
- Understands more familiar one-part directions, such as "Get
  the ball" and "Give it to me"
- Can point to nose, eyes, and mouth upon request
- Points to familiar objects and people when asked ("Where's
  Mama?")
- May shake head "no" in refusal or protest
- Pushes adult away, fusses, or whines when mad or upset
- Nonverbally shows excitement, surprise, and recognition
  through smiling and laughing
- May have anywhere from two to eight real words in his ex-
  pressive vocabulary (one word may mean several things)
- Uses jargon talk, or gibberish, which *sounds* like he is talking
  in phrases or sentences, yet is difficult to comprehend

Motor Skills

- Climbs onto furniture; tries to climb out of crib or highchair
- Climbs stairs on all fours
- Stoops and picks up a toy

- Is very active; runs rapidly, stops, and starts again, going from one activity to the next
- Experiments by walking backwards
- Can hold two small toys in one hand simultaneously
- Can throw a ball from a standing or sitting position

Toy Play

- Turns the pages of a book and looks at the pictures
- Functional toy play begins—imitates brushing doll's hair or stirring in a cup
- Puts pegs in a pegboard
- Rolls a ball back and forth
- Holds a crayon and scribbles with wide-sweeping movements
- Likes to find an object hidden inside or underneath another object
- Enjoys playing with household articles that he has seen adults use: cups, pots, pans, spoons, tools, keys, and anything found in a typical American junk drawer
- Enjoys dumping and pouring sand or water
- Adores musical toys and rhythm instruments
- Likes to push/pull, pile, knock down, empty, and fill

Playtime Activities

Finger Plays

Finger plays provide fun, mutual interaction with your child, which gives him yet another opportunity to socialize with you, and encourages his attempts at trying out new words and motor movements. Most children continue to enjoy finger plays up until they are four years old. The younger child does not pay attention to getting his fingers right, but rather is more attentive

How big is Erin? Sooo big.

to the rhythm and music that serve to carry the words. For the older child, finger plays present a new challenge. It is not unusual to see three-year-olds sing while concentrating quite intently on putting each gesture and movement in the right order. With practice, finger plays become almost automatic, yet most children still enjoy repeating them over and over again.

Place your child in his high chair, or on the floor, sitting directly across from you. Sing the following verses in a lively, animated voice.

Bees in a Beehive
Bees in a beehive, where are the bees? [make a fist, wave from side to side]
Hidden inside where nobody sees [with other hand, point to beehive]
Soon they come creeping, out of the hive [creep with fingers]
One, two, three, four, five! [release fingers, one at a time]

Your child may use gibberish along with the song, or begin a crude copying of your hand and finger movements. Show him how pleased you are with his participation. Showing your approval makes baby feel that his play is worthwhile and that you are proud of his efforts.

Sound Play

Babies naturally engage in sound play in the early months of life, vocalizing to themselves for the pleasure and stimulation it provides. Later, baby is capable of watching you directly and more consciously imitating vocal sounds and words for the fun and challenge that the social exchange offers.

While baby is seated in his high chair, and at your eye level, demonstrate several lip positions and encourage him to imitate you. The following positions are preliminary speech movements which he will later use in his production of real words.

1. Round your lips and blow out, placing baby's hand in front of your mouth to feel the air. Tear up tissue paper and blow it around on his tray. Blow Ping-Pong balls or feathers across baby's tray and see if he will try to copy your movements of lip rounding.
2. Say each vowel, one at a time, and see if baby will copy you. Vary the pitch of your repetitions (e-e-e-e) and go up and down the pitch range slowly, holding baby's attention to your face. Does he try to copy the sounds or facial expressions you make?
3. Next, pair two different sounds together as in "uh oh," "ee-oh," or "i-ee" and see if he attempts to match your sounds. Wait for him to respond to you before trying again. String together nonsense sounds and make up silly songs, such as "bee bi bee, bee bi bo, I love you, oh oh oh."

Some babies demonstrate a very keen interest in faces and will readily copy the actions and oral motor movements of an adult. Others will stare intently at the adult's facial expressions, mouthing the oral motor movements as if they're not conscious of being caught up in the game!

All My Toys

Gather up a few of baby's favorite toys and place them in a paper bag. Sit facing each other on the floor and ask baby, "What's in the bag?" As he reaches for the bag, suddenly open it and let him pick out a toy. Quickly close the bag and name the toy, being very animated in your expressions: "Block. There's your block." Pause and see if he will imitate the name.

Go through the game once again and ask baby the questions, letting him pull out a toy. Once you have two or three items on the floor, point to one and say, "What's that?" If he

"What's inside the bag?"

doesn't attempt to answer after a few moments, name it for him saying, "Oh, that's your truck. Justin's truck."

In this game, baby is learning the names of his toys and is given an opportunity to try to say the names as well. If he says nothing, don't be discouraged. At least he is hearing you speak the names and is learning what the toys are. He will attempt naming them in the months to come, or when he is ready.

It is not necessary to buy an array of expensive toys for your baby's enjoyment. You can use simple, everyday objects (spoon, comb, tea strainer, keys, etc.) in this game, which he will explore with interest.

As for buying new toys, it is better to introduce a few at a time than bombard him with a confusing variety of toys all at once. Get the most mileage out of his toys by occasionally putting familiar ones away for awhile and bringing them back out in a few weeks. He will treat them as if they're brand new!

Animal Talk

Most children love animals and are fascinated by their playful antics. Animals provide children with a sense of caring that is unconditionally reciprocated, like when baby strokes the kitty and is rewarded with gentle nuzzling or provoked into playing a game of chase.

If you have a dog or cat in your home and call it by name, chances are your baby understands its name too. In fact, the name of your beloved pet will most likely be one of the first words in your baby's expressive repertoire (besides mama and daddy, of course).

Begin to point out other animals, naming them for baby and making the animal sounds. There are many baby books on the market that feature animals. Pick one that has wipeable stiff pages and no more than two animals per page. Point to the animal, name it, and make the sound: "Cow. That's a cow. The cow says, moooooo"; "Kitty. See the kitty. Meow, meow"; "Horse. Ride the horse. Neigh, neigh."

Soon baby will be able to associate the name with the picture of the animal. When he starts to talk about an animal, he may name the cow by saying, "moooo," using the sound instead of the word. That's alright; when learning new words, baby will zero in on that which attracts his attention the most. Since the vowels are drawn out on "mooooo," compared to the single syllabled "cow," baby's attention is attracted to the former, so that his representation of the animal is characterized by the sound it makes.

Television commercials present the same type of salient features, attracting and holding baby's attention to a greater extent than the programs themselves. Commercials are not only broadcast louder, but are designed to attract the attention of the viewer by using highly inflected speech patterns and snappy music.

Container Play

Earlier, your toddler learned how to grasp and hold onto objects, and, later, he figured out how to let go of an object when he wanted to. Grasping, picking up, and letting go of an object are all different skills, and, with a little practice, become perfected and orchestrated into smooth, efficient movements.

Set a container between you and baby and take turns dropping objects inside. Small blocks and pegs are good, or use objects of different weights and sizes so that he learns to associate the noise with the object as it hits the bottom of the container. If he is not sure how to let go of the object, show him by putting the block in your hand and spreading your fingers wide as you drop the toy.

Tell him what you are doing: "Drop the block; block goes *in* the cup. Now let's put *all* the blocks in the cup. We did it! Can you take them out?" Dropping is an exciting new skill for tod-

My favorite game: container play.

dlers, and they may practice it over and over again out of pure
enjoyment for the activity.

Container play is a good prerequisite skill in learning to
help clean up. With your assistance, it is not too early to guide
your toddler to help pick up his toys at the end of the day and
put them in his toybox: "Let's put the toys away, Justin. Help
Mommy."

Pick up a toy from the floor and hand it to him while pointing to the toybox. He may need your assistance at first (walk him to the box, guide his hand and tell him to drop). After watching a few demonstrations from you, he will get the idea and may help with his toys on a routine basis.

This does not mean, however, that he has learned that everything has its place! At this point, your toddler enjoys emptying and dropping simply for their own sake. It isn't until he's around two years old that emptying becomes part of a larger plan, like trying to find a specific object in a container full of toys. For now, the 13- to 15-month-old will enjoy emptying everything possible of being emptied—magazine racks, ashtrays, sewing baskets, coffee cans, and your purse, if you're not careful.

Hide-and-Seek

Your baby is continuing to make great gains in his perception of how things work in his world. He now recognizes familiar objects, even when they're presented in unusual positions. For example, when you hand him a picture book upside down, he turns it right side up. He knows that other people and objects are separate from him, and he begins to make important associations or connections with objects. In addition, his idea of cause and effect is expanding. He knows that just because an object is covered does not mean that it has disappeared completely. If you cover his toy with a napkin, he quickly retrieves it and recognizes the napkin as the cause of his inability to see the toy. He is thinking logically about the world.

Challenge this ability by going a step further. First, hide a small toy under a hat a couple of times and each time ask him to find it. Then use another cover, for instance, a cup turned upside down. As he watches, place the toy under the cup. At first, he may look under the hat, because this is where he made his original association. Show him where the toy is and play the game a few more times until he makes the differentiation.

Give your child many opportunities to play with toys that have barriers (a toy that hides behind another object). The barrier may be a flap, lid, or door that can be opened or closed.

Household objects with barriers that a child may enjoy include: a tackle box, window blinds, crackers in a box, a pocketbook, and toys in plastic containers with lids. Commercial toys include those with doors that slide or pull open (Fisher-Price house and barn sets), shape boxes with screw tops, and stuffed animals with pouches.

Such "barrier" games are fun, and toddlers love the excitement of finding something hidden. Be sure to show enthusiasm while you play, naming the objects and describing your actions. When baby lifts the correct barrier, exaggerate your expressions. "There it is; Justin found it! *Under* the hat!"

String Pull

Another activity to strengthen your child's intellect is the "String Pull." Now you are interested in determining if baby comprehends tool use, that is, using a tool or object to obtain a toy, rather than grabbing the toy at first sight. Babies love pulling on strings, and at first will need some time to simply play with the string in their own way.

Seated at the kitchen table, set baby on your lap so you are both facing the tabletop. Place two shoestrings in front of him to play with. Let him pick them up and twist, turn, pull, and generally explore them until he's satisfied. Next, tie a toy on the end of one string and put the toy at the far end of the table so he must pull the string in order to get it. Discourage him from simply grabbing the toy. Show him how pulling the string brings the toy closer and within reach.

Now encourage him to get the toy, by way of the string, all by himself. Say, "Pull the string, Justin. Here comes the toy. Pull some more. Here it comes. Pull some more. There, you did it!"

Impart to him the feeling of anticipation when giving your directions, but follow his lead. He may get the toy in one quick pull.

Next, let him play with both shoestrings, and observe his discovery that only one string will bring him the toy. He has made a connection in his mind, and that is that the string can be used as a means to an end; pulling the string gets him the toy.

Give baby the opportunity to practice this skill in other locations, such as on the floor or in his highchair. Initially his interest may focus on the string, then on the toy, and finally he will see the connection between the two as he experiments.

Ball Roll

Play baby's first game of catch. Sit on the floor, legs apart, with baby sitting between them, and have another person sit

"I caught it!"

facing you a short distance away. Show baby how to roll the ball to the other person, saying, "Roll the ball, Justin. Roll it to Daddy." He may push it a short distance, or accidentally flick it with his hand. Treat this action as purposeful, saying, "There. You rolled the ball. Let's do it again, Daddy's turn."

Try different sizes of balls: tennis balls versus large beach balls. Vary the game by running toy cars and trucks back and forth to each other, emphasizing that you are taking turns in the game, and making sounds that accompany your play ("Rrrrmm-mmm, here comes the car, get ready, here it comes"). You may gradually increase the distance between you so that baby can learn to improve his accuracy and aim.

Most importantly, you are teaching baby turn-taking behavior in the interaction, and he learns to anticipate what comes next in the sequence of play actions. Enjoy ball play with all family members seated on the floor with baby, making it a three- or four-way game. Ask him to roll the ball to a specific person: "Roll the ball to Grandpa, Justin. Good. Here it comes again. Now roll the ball to Mommy."

In time, baby will shift from rolling and throwing to bouncing and catching balls of various sizes.

Toy Wrap

The 14-month-old's sense of exploration and discovery is immense. He will sit for long periods fascinated by leaves blowing in the wind outside his window. And he wants to handle and investigate anything within reach, mechanical objects holding a special interest for him (knobs on the TV and radio, and doorknobs).

A fun activity to challenge his investigative prowess is "Toy Wrap." Loosely wrap a small object or toy in tissue paper while your baby watches, and leave part of the toy visible. Give him plenty of time to unwrap the toy before you give assistance. Say, "What's inside, Justin? Get it out! Wow, you did it!" Encourage

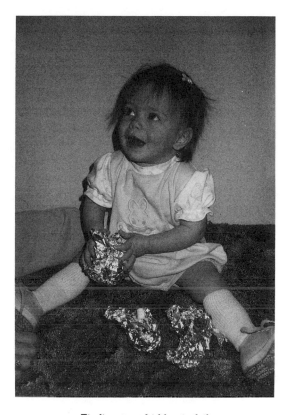

Finding toys hidden in foil.

baby to unwrap his birthday and Christmas gifts. (Show him how to pull and tear, and help him with the taped ends.)

To make it a bit more difficult, wrap a toy or cookie in shiny aluminum foil, which conforms to the shape of the object and is more challenging to remove. Upon removing the object, ask, "What's that? What did you find?" and see if he'll try to name it. He learns the names of things by hearing you name them for him time and time again. Eventually, he will try saying the names, either when he has the need to, or when he discovers the power of words to get what he wants. *Note:* Be careful not to drill him. If he doesn't respond after one questioning, simply continue playing in a nonjudgmental manner. He may name the toy out of anticipatory surprise after unwrapping it; or he may not say anything at all.

Naming objects in and of itself is not a predictor of intelligence or an isolated goal to assure you that your child is brighter than other 15-month-olds. Some children are labelers, running around and pointing to things they see and naming them out loud. This is their style of interacting with the world. Others well understand the names of objects in their environment, but see no need to name them (unless of course they want something, in which case naming becomes a very functional tool).

Smelling Flowers

Babies have a fully developed sense of smell at birth. Many of our early experiences and memories in childhood are linked to familiar and provoking odors, like a chocolate cake baking in the oven, a freshly cut Christmas tree, Dad's after-shave lotion. Bring your toddler's attention to the various odors in his world by describing the sensation, giving you both the opportunity to enjoy the aroma.

Bring freshly cut flowers into your home, or stroll through a garden and smell the flowers. Let your child touch the flowers and put them to his nose. Take a deep breath and smell loudly! "Ummmm, that smells good. Justin, smell. Flowers smell *soooo* good."

Introduce your child to smells in the kitchen—cinnamon sticks, onions, ginger, lemon. Call his attention to the aromas of fresh-baked bread, simmering spaghetti sauce, and steaming hot chocolate. Expose him to different flavor concentrates you may have in your cupboard, like vanilla, peppermint extract, lemon juice, and garlic.

Exaggerate the action of smelling at first so that he can

better understand how to breathe in through his nose. Tell him how you think something smells, calling his attention to scents and odors in your everyday encounters: "Ooh, yummy, that smells *sooo* good"; "Can you smell that, Justin? Yuk, that smells rotten. Pee yew!"

Activities in Your Daily Routines of Dressing, Feeding, and Bathing Your Baby

Get the Shirt

Before dressing your toddler, lie his clothes on the floor, a few feet away from both of you. Point to the pile of clothes and say, "Time to get dressed. Where's your shirt? Go get your shirt." Once he picks it up and brings it to you, show how excited you are that he followed your directions.

Ask him to retrieve the remaining items one by one. If he doesn't understand the name of an item (pants, for example), pick it up and name it while his attention is on you. Make a fun game out of it by hiding the pants under the bed and asking, "Where are your pants?" as he watches. Encourage him to get the pants and bring them to you.

Try to be conscious of allowing your toddler the opportunity to assist in the dressing process. A child enjoys carrying out simple directions and feels he is an important part of the routine when he realizes he can help. Try not to have all his clothing items ready ahead of time, but let him see you take them out as you name them, or enlist his help in finding an item.

I Want More

Set your toddler up in his high chair and tell him it's "time to eat." Put only a few morsels of his favorite finger food (for example, a piece of cheese, Cheerios) on the tray so that he needs to ask for more. When he's finished eating and looks down to his empty tray, he may extend his arms and whine in request for "more." If so, hold up a piece of food next to your face (so he can see how the word is formed on your lips) and ask, "More? Justin wants more?" Pause and observe his excitement or gesturing to indicate his desire for more. As you give him more food, repeatedly say, "Here's more. More cheese for Justin."

Later, when he is pounding on the tray for more, say, "You want more? Tell me, 'more.'" Emphasize the word "more" in your sentence. Wait for him to attempt saying the word, but don't take him to the point of frustration. If he tries to say the word (in whatever form), praise him for his efforts and immediately give him the food. Accept any sound combination he uses for "more." Perhaps he will say "da da da" as he reaches out, asking for more. He has realized that talking will get him what he wants, whereas crying and fussing were earlier forms of communicating his needs to you. If he continues to cry and fuss, discontinue the game and try again later.

In this exercise, you are encouraging your baby to test out the power of words. He soon comes to understand that instead of crying or whining he can obtain a desired food or object by telling you what he wants.

Hot and Cold

Note: Do not leave a baby unattended or available to play with a faucet on his own.

Fill the tub with water, about two inches deep, and place your baby in a sitting position facing the faucet. Turn the faucet on cold and encourage baby to let the water run over his hands while you say, "Oh, the water's *cold*. *Cold* water, brrr." Next, adjust the water to a warmer temperature (not too hot to harm or scald the child) and say, "Oh, my, water is *hot*. *Hot* water," emphasizing the descriptive word "hot." Pause and see if baby will imitate the word.

Over the next several months, continue describing the temperature of the water and occasionally ask baby how the water feels. Eventually, he will say the words by himself when he feels the hot and cold temperatures, understanding and verbalizing "hot" first.

Think of other descriptive words you could be using during bathtime, such as wet and dry, soft and warm (while toweling); or fast and slow, sink and float (while playing with bath toys).

Using a Spoon

Expecting messiness is the first rule of thumb when letting your child eat with a spoon. First, let him play with an extra spoon while you are feeding him. He will tap the tray, bring the spoon to your mouth, dabble in the food, and simply experiment.

When you're ready to let him spoon-feed independently, give him a bowl of food that will stick to the spoon; this makes it easier to get the food to his mouth in one piece! Put your hand on his and guide the spoon if necessary. He will hold the spoon in his fist and may dump the contents on his tray occasionally. It will take some practice to coordinate turning his wrist for hand to mouth movements.

Show him how pleased you are with his efforts at spoon-feeding. "My, Justin, you're eating with a spoon. Look at you!" When he is finished, ask him to give you the spoon, then the cup, from his tray. See if he picks each of them out as you name them. Give him a variety of spoons (big, small, wooden) to play with while you are preparing his meal, so that he has the opportunity to manipulate and explore them *before* feeding time.

Stimulation Techniques

Now that your baby is beginning to use real words in his communication, you can help him along by modeling the cor-

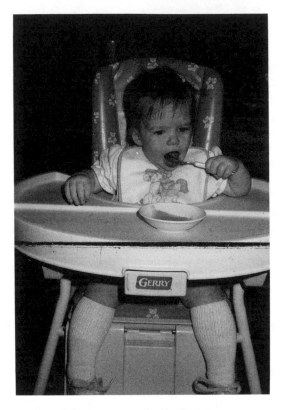

Using a spoon for the first time.

rect word that you think he is trying to say. If he says, "Ah da" as he shoves his empty bowl towards you, you can then say, "All done," so that he immediately hears the correct way to say the words and is acknowledged for his attempts.

He is trying very hard to communicate complete thoughts with just one word or several sounds, therefore, his word attempts may often perplex you. If it is difficult to understand what he is trying to say, make a guess at the meaning of his utterance and put it into his own words. If baby says "du" as he reaches for his cup, you can ask, "Juice?" and see if your guess is correct. Soon you will see that baby is developing his own consistent sound combinations for words ("du" always means "juice"), which Mom and Dad just need to figure out!

There are two things you can be sure of in regard to your toddler's acquisition of language: (1) he will demonstrate an understanding of many words and phrases *before* he will begin to use them; and (2) he will intentionally use whatever language he has available to him to affect the behavior of others.

The one-year-old has a mind of his own. No longer will he be content sitting and watching you gaze into his eyes and chattering away like you used to do when he was three months old. He understands and reacts to many more words now, and is eager to act upon them, sometimes in contrast to his parent's desires. On a trip to the grocery store, he tries to squirm out of the basket seat to stand and points to objects on the shelf, eager to explore the displays of items. At home he empties magazine racks and turns the pages, jargoning to himself as he heads for another basket to empty, without regard for putting items back to their proper place. However, he does understand that his actions affect another's behavior toward him, and he also realizes just how to use language to make an impression on others.

Your child feels the power of social language; he knows he can get your attention by pulling at your leg, crying, poking, hugging, yelling, or showing off. But he also learns that his ability to have an effect on you has its limits. He can whine and fuss, push you away, and jargon all he wants with a demanding tone of voice, yet you will finish changing his diaper despite the protests.

Another by-product of your child's growing self-awareness is his rudimentary sense of humor. He understands that he can become the center of attention and enjoys the applause after a performance. He may dance in the middle of the room, flail his arms, turn in circles, and plop to the floor. After scanning the room for your approval, he gets up and starts the exact routine all over again, enjoying the role of the entertainer.

Your child's growing mental abilities, exploratory behaviors, and use of language enable him to become more of an active member of the family. His drive and excitement for learning requires much tolerance and patience on the part of family members, while he practices and masters new skills.

CHAPTER SEVEN

Understanding Language
16–18 Months

From infancy, your child has been like a little computer, storing up information and building on her past experiences which make up her receptive understanding of the world. Her receptive language, or understanding of words and concepts, is learned in the context of her everyday routines with you at home.

As early as nine months of age, babies learn to follow simple directions. When you say, "Come here, Sarah," and stretch out your arms to receive her, she responds by crawling to you. She arrived at this understanding of the direction based on your tone of voice, body movements (arms outstretched), and facial expressions in your communication to her. Several months later, you could give the same direction without the additional cues of body movements and facial expressions (if you were out of sight, in another room), and she would understand the direction based on your words alone.

Another simple direction babies learn early is "Give it to me." If baby has a toy in her hand, and you say, "Give it to Mommy," holding your hand out and gesturing to her, she learns very quickly that she is expected to release the toy into your hand. By 16 months, accompanying gestures are no longer necessary; baby understands what you have asked of her because she now comprehends the words.

Your child's comprehension of new vocabulary words and simple directions continues to expand, and she relies less on gestures and more on words to derive meaning. At the same time she begins naming objects, she also starts to form general concepts in her mind and groups things into categories. In time, she learns that a ball may be hard or soft, green or red, big or small, but that all balls share the common use of being thrown or rolled in a game.

Before she learns this concept, however, she may call the moon an apple, or name anything else that is round a "ball." This over-extension of word meanings is sometimes quite amusing. Has your child ever greeted every bearded man she sees as "Daddy?" (provided Daddy has a beard), or called every four-legged animal a "doggie?" Your toddler is making some very important connections in her mind regarding the meaning of words and phrases at this time. Soon her generalizations will become more specific, and the number and category of words she understands will flourish.

Parents are often concerned when they notice that a new word that the child has used for weeks is suddenly dropped and appears to have been forgotten. This is very typical of the 1½-year-old; a child's vocabulary at this stage of development fluctuates, and word meanings are not yet completely fixed in the child's mind.

Keep in mind that children progress through the stages of language development in a zigzag fashion, and in spurts and starts, with much variability from child to child. Some children use a single word to mean many things for quite some time. Others abound in jargon interspersed with single words, and still others use a word constantly, only to drop it and discontinue using it for quite some time. Giving your child a word for each new feeling or encounter she experiences will ensure the growth of her vocabulary and conceptual skills in the months to come.

Developmental Milestones

Understanding and Talking

- Understands short and simple sentences
- Comprehends and enjoys rhymes and songs
- Follows a simple command like, "Give me the cup"
- Understands many more words than she can say
- Recognizes and points to several body parts
- May be using 10–20 words expressively (words may come and go)
- Uses a question inflection in her speech ("huh?")
- Repeats words after adults
- Still uses jargon in her conversation
- Enjoys picture books, labels pictures, and turns the pages
- Protests by saying "no"
- Uses greetings such as "hi" and "bye-bye"
- Names objects she sees (says "doggie" while pointing to an animal)
- Shows varied facial expressions of emotions (anger, fear, affection, sympathy, joy, anxiety)
- Explores the environment more independently when a familiar person is nearby
- Likes to "help" do easy chores

Motor Skills

- Runs, although somewhat stiffly
- Walks down stairs holding onto adult's hand for assistance
- Can stand on one foot while holding adult's hand
- Can walk up stairs, using a railing
- Can kneel on both knees without support
- Uses thumb and first finger to pick up small objects

Toy Play

- Likes to unwrap toys or find ones hidden
- On a simple shape puzzle board, can take out and fit in the circle
- Shows tool use (uses a stick or string to reach a desired toy)
- Enjoys stacking blocks
- Gives toy to adult if unable to operate
- Pretends to feed a doll and comb its hair
- Scribbles with crayon or marker
- Fills push/pull toys with multiple objects
- Enjoys hidden-object toys; soft, lightweight stuffed toys; simple pop-up toys activated by pushing a button or knob; nesting cups; and pounding bench

Playtime Activities

Telephone Talk

While you are on the telephone, occasionally give your toddler the opportunity to listen to the person with whom you are speaking. Try it with someone the child knows well, such as grandma or a neighbor friend.

First, let your toddler hold the phone and listen to the dial tone. At first she may explore both ends before putting it to her ear. Then, let her listen to the speaker. She will be amazed at the special voice she hears, so much so that she most likely will not say anything.

Place a toy telephone next to the real one and role play with your toddler, going through the motions of dialing, saying "hello," and having a simple conversation. Keep the dialogue short and simple, talking about the here and now.

You can also set up toy phone play with your toddler and one of her stuffed animals. Observe how she holds the phone to her ear and then switches to the animal's ear, perhaps chattering away in the process. She now understands that ears are for

"Hello Daddy, how are you?"

listening, and can pretend telephone play with her dolls and stuffed animals.

Children should be encouraged to listen to others, not only for receiving information and instructions, but also out of courtesy to others. Learning to listen is a learned skill, one that develops over a long period of time. For now, though, be brief. Introduce the telephone, but supervise it properly. Your child will learn the standards for appropriate telephone behavior by watching you, so, in your role playing, remember to listen attentively, talk politely (and briefly), and say goodbye before you hang up.

Scrap Book

Now is a good time for your toddler to have her very own book of pictures, handmade by you, with pictures of familiar objects and people. This is very useful in expanding the child's vocabulary and she will be proud to show off her very own book.

Paste photographs of all family members, pets, common objects, and toys on large sheets of paper stapled together. Have the child point to pictures as you name them, or ask her to find a picture and see if she can remember where it is located in the book.

Four or five pages is enough for now, but once she can easily identify and begins naming familiar pictures, cut out pictures of new "words" from magazines and add pages to her book. Begin to teach her words that she does not yet understand; you will be amazed at how quickly her vocabulary grows.

During this period of word labeling, a parent's intervention is quite important. Studies have shown that disadvantaged children have significantly raised their IQ scores when the parents were instructed to read books and label objects for their children. In another study, children who were exposed to caregivers who labeled objects and talked about experiences to them developed more advanced speech skills than those who did not receive added stimulation. Because verbal skills are so highly valued in our society today, providing this type of stimulation is worth the effort. *Note:* If you have a video cassette recorder, "photo books" depicting real actions of a child at play are also a valuable learning tool.

Tumble Time

At 16 months, your toddler may be predominantly motor-driven, that is, interested in crawling over low barriers, throwing balls, carrying toys while walking, and climbing up and down the stairs. (Walking up and down the stairs is alright, with your help.)

Rolling and tumbling on the floor with your child will be enthusiastically received. Play a game of "roly poly," attaching words to her actions. Lie down flat on the floor and roll from one end of the room to the other, like a steamroller. Roll toward each other, and purposely make contact, saying "bump, bump, bump!" (Gently please, fathers.)

Other fun movements for your child to imitate include: standing on tiptoes as you say, "Stand tall"; pretending to climb a mountain, saying, "We're climbing, we're climbing"; and squatting down, head tucked in, holding your knees, saying, "Let's make a ball." Shake your head, bounce your shoulders, swing your arms, stamp your feet—encourage her to try them all.

Your toddler (and older siblings, too) will love imitating your movements; the more active you are, the better. Acting out motions and attaching words to them helps your child learn action words (verbs) which describe her movements.

Balloon Fun

Now that baby is walking independently (although, perhaps somewhat awkwardly), provide another challenge that will encourage her to bat at a suspended object while standing. Tie three balloons each on the end of a string, and tape the ends of the strings to the ceiling so that the balloons are floating about one foot above the floor. Gently swat at the balloons and watch their delicate motion.

Encourage baby to pat the balloons and set them into motion. Watching the balloons float and bump each other provides fascination for baby. She learns to experiment by hitting the balloons lightly, then harder, and observes the different movements. Balloons move slowly through the air so that baby can easily track their motions.

Describe your actions as you play: "Pat the balloon, Sarah. Whew, it went way up. Here it comes. Bump, bump. Bump the balloons. Wheee!"

Older children, two years old and up, enjoy kicking sus-

Batting balloons.

pended balloons. Kicking requires that the child be able to stand
on one foot for a few seconds, which is good practice in learning
how to balance.

Piano Player

If you have a piano in your home, no doubt you have observed your child imitating an older sister's sonatas (well, not

quite) and pounding away for the sheer fun of it. Toddlers at this age still enjoy exploring by poking, tapping, pounding, and even tasting things, just to see what happens. And what better reinforcement for all this experimentation than musical notes, which can be soft or loud, and high or low.

Purchase a small toy piano and show your toddler how to place her fingers on the keys. Let her play on her own for awhile, then show her how to tap a key with one finger. (That's a challenge!)

Later, extend this activity into pretend play, without the piano as a prop: "Sarah, let's play piano." Pretend to be playing on the edge of a table, moving your fingers vigorously. As your toddler imitates, sing, "Play, play, play. Play, play, play. Play the piano, play, play, play," in any tune you wish. It won't be long before she starts imitating your words (perhaps saying "pay" for "play"). She will learn many new words in simple rhythms and songs; simple ones that you make up are the best.

Purse Play

The world is full of so many kinds of containers—what is a child to do? Children up to three years old find emptying and filling containers, and exploring the contents in the process, a very interesting activity.

Provide your toddler with an old purse that she can carry around in her play. Place inside it everyday, grown-up items that are safe for her to explore. Include a set of keys, a comb, tissues, and a small change purse. (Forget the lipstick if you value your walls!) Describe her actions as she explores the contents: "Keys. Sarah found the keys. What else is in your purse?"

She will feel important imitating mother's scenario, although her play episodes will be brief. Children this age begin to pretend by using common objects they've observed their parents using on a daily basis. For example, your toddler may take the comb out of the purse, pretend to comb her hair, and put the

"A purse of my own."

comb back in. She is on her way to the development of more imaginative play, where she will sequence actions based on a creative thought process.

One, Two, Three

How many times during the day do you have the opportunity to count items as you give them to your toddler? Why not take advantage of the time you do have and make an effort to play a game of "One, two, three." Your child will not be actually learning to count, but will begin to imitate your words. "Number" words are also new vocabulary that she hasn't been exposed to before.

At snack time, count out cookies or raisins as you hand them to her. For starters, just count up to three; then pause, and

Let's count the crackers.

count up to three again. Remember to use lots of sing-song in your voice, since your toddler is still attentive to the pitch, tone, and rhythm of your speech. Soon, she will begin imitating your counting. Even though the words will not be pronounced exactly right, they will sound very much like "one, two, three" because of the inflection.

Counting material is readily available. Try buttons on a sweater, fingers and toes, blocks and toys, steps in a flight of stairs, silverware at mealtime, and shoes in mother's closet.

It is humorous to observe children in the early preschool years begin to master the steps toward learning numbers. Although the child knows to recite numbers, she may not do so in the proper order. Thus, "one, two, three, fiftyleven, seventeen" may be a typical child-invented sequence that is used over and over again. A two-year-old may be able to count to ten, but when asked to count four blocks, she's stumped. At this age,

counting indicates good rote memory, but not a true understanding of what numbers are for.

All Gone

The 18-month-old understands the meaning of many words
before she begins using them. Still using mostly jargon and
gestures to communicate, she gradually uses more real words
and enjoys using several two syllable phrases (such as bye-bye,
all gone, and thank you) with enthusiasm.

Encourage the use of "all gone" during mealtime. When
she has finished her juice, turn her cup upside down and say,
"All gone." If she picks up the cup and looks at you quizzically,
ask, "Sarah, where's the juice?" Wait for her to answer. If she
doesn't, say, "Juice, all gone" in a highly inflected tone of voice.

Follow up this activity by playing a hide-and-find game
with a small toy. While she's watching, hide the toy behind your
back and ask, "Where did it go?" Exaggerate your gestures and
gaze around the floor for the toy: "Car's all gone. All gone, car.
Can you find it?"

Some children may not combine two words at a time until
their vocabulary reaches well over 100 words. The child may
need to make some important connections in her mind before
linking together a series of words. Other children use two-word
phrases as early as 16 months.

Scribble Art

Learning to draw is a developmental process that can be
encouraged by introducing children to drawing materials early,
and letting them scribble and experiment. The goal is not to
teach the child to draw anything in particular, as she will learn

Scribbling all around.

the skill of drawing at her own rate, and will go through many developmental steps before the skill is acquired.

Tape a sheet of paper to your toddler's tray and give her an oversized crayon. A large crayon will fit nicely in her hand as she practices and develops the fine motor coordination required to make marks on the page. Make wide strokes on the paper and then let her try. At first she will be quite fascinated and enjoy filling the whole sheet of paper with her scribbles. The lines will be wavy and dark as she practices grossly moving her arm forward and backward. Later, the scribbles will turn into circles, and, by the time she is two, will develop into more differentiated forms and shapes.

Switch crayons with her so that she can scribble with various colors. Describe her actions: "Sarah can color. Here's your crayon. It's blue. The color blue. I like blue." Hang her scribble art on the refrigerator at her eye level so she can view it from time to time. It's not too early to emphasize that crayons are for coloring on paper *only*. Always supervise your child when doing any kind of art activity.

Thank You!

Your child is very attentive and aware of the various social exchanges going on around her. The check-out clerk at the grocery store catches her eye and says hi; the pastor at the church waves and says bye as she's whisked away in daddy's arms; the woman at day care says thank you when baby hands her the cup for more milk. Children learn to label these social exchanges very early on, and will imitate the words appropriately when given models in their everyday lives.

Your child's expressive vocabulary will continue to grow in leaps and bounds from 18 months on. Her favorite words may consist of two syllables (bye-bye, uh oh, all gone), which she uses emphatically to get your attention and comment on the events in her world. Another easy two-syllable word that will soon become part of her active vocabulary is "thank you."

Whenever you request your toddler to give you something, remember to say, "thank you." It won't be long before she will begin imitating you, using other sounds that she is capable of making ("ta tu"), but you'll understand what she means. Even when you hand her an object, say "thank you," providing yet another model of the phrase for her.

Activities in Your Daily Routines of Dressing, Feeding, and Bathing Your Baby

Whose Shoes?

At this point, your child will most likely understand whose shoes belong to who in the family, although she may delight in putting on Daddy's shoes herself and flopping around the

Where are Daddy's shoes?

Do you want milk or juice?

house. Test her ability to differentiate between the different pairs and recognize the ownership of mommy's versus daddy's.

With several pairs of shoes within sight of both of you, ask her, "Where are Mommy's shoes? Go get Mommy's shoes, please." Can she follow your directions and bring you the right pair?

As you are dressing her each day, ask your toddler to get her shoes and bring them to you. In doing so, you are giving her more independence in her dressing and helping her to assume a small dose of responsibility. Soon it will be her job to pick out her own clothes, and having her seek out and bring these items to you one at a time is a beginning step to the goal of independent dressing. On the way to this goal, she learns the names of clothing items, as well as how to follow your directions.

Giving Choices

During mealtime, you can give your toddler the opportunity to make a choice between foods and reinforce her attempts at trying to indicate her desire using words. Say, "Sarah, do you want milk or juice?" Show her the two items as you ask the question; then wait for her response. If she points to one, encourage her to verbalize also by acknowledging her request and saying, "Juice, you want juice." If she attempts to say the word (says "du" for juice), hug and praise her for using speech by saying, "Juice, you said juice, Sarah's talking!" and give her the juice.

If she does not attempt to say the word, and points to what she wants, give it to her and continue to model your actions by saying, "Here's your juice, Sarah. Yumm, juice is good."

Tub Toys

Near the tub, keep a bucket of colorful plastic toys that your toddler can enjoy during her bath. Especially fun and interesting are large and small boats, a container of bubbles, large spoons and scoops, sponges, and containers for dumping and pouring water. Talk about what your toddler is doing, as she is doing it. Give her the experience of learning the descriptive words that match her actions.

Action	*Words*
Pouring and dumping out water	"You *poured* water *into* the cup." "Now the cup is *full*." "Let's *dump* the water *out*."
Blowing bubbles	"Watch me *blow* bubbles." "They go way up *high*." "Can you *pop* the bubbles?"

Squeezing a sponge   *"Squeeze* the sponge."
                              "It's *full* of water."
                              "Let's *squeeze* the water *out.*"

Sleepy Time

Your walking, talking, great bundle of energy has kept you entertained and hopping for the past 12 hours. When it's time for sleep, she may fuss a little (all kids do), or get all wound up and excitable in an attempt to prevent the inevitable bedtime routine. Many children this age require about 12 hours of sleep per night, in addition to an hourly afternoon nap, in order to function pleasantly throughout the day.

Always warn her 10 or 15 minutes in advance that soon it will be bedtime. If she's playing with toys, tell her you'll help her put them away in order to get ready for bed. Make the transition a quiet one by reading a book, or telling a story. Although it's often frustrating, refrain from demanding and yelling; this will only serve to excite her even more.

Once she is settled in bed, hold her hand, or lay your hand comfortably on her back or chest. Remain there, silently watching her, until she falls asleep. In this stillness, you are free from distractions and can appreciate the joy and tremendous beauty your child brings to you. This quiet contact time is very simple, but powerful.

It is interesting to take a step back and reflect on the changes in your child's development over the past 18 months. Observing the transition from an infant who had cycled in and out of dozing states to a child who has her own set of likes and dislikes, plus the verbal ability to express them, you can more fully realize and appreciate the astonishing growth and change that has taken place. As you watch these changes on a day-to-day basis, they are difficult to recognize and appreciate. But, over time, there is a slow accumulation of small transformations so that the child you observed a month ago is quite changed from the child you are observing now. Taking the time to appreciate the natural beauty and growth of your child slows the world down a bit, at least until morning, when her silent stillness again turns into an active ball of energy.

Stimulation Techniques

As you have gathered, in almost all of the activities, you are being encouraged to talk to your child. This does not mean you have to talk constantly; certainly you will want to share quiet times together as well, and constant chatter becomes very boring. By using "self-talk"—describing what you are doing, seeing, or feeling as you carry out an activity—you are building your child's vocabulary and teaching her much more about her world than she takes in visually.

If your child attends a day care facility, take the time to observe the interactions going on there between your child and the caregiver. Does the caregiver kneel down to the child's eye level when speaking with her? Does she listen to your child with patience and encourage her desire to communicate? Is she tuned into your child's personality and feelings, or are the child's physical needs being met adequately without much meaningful interaction? The suggestion that language problems are inherent in day care settings is certainly not being suggested here. What is suggested is that inattentive day care providers are not acceptable caregivers for young children. Centers that focus mainly on rigid structuring and physical control of children, rather than individual expression and play, do not contribute greatly to a child's language development.

Listening and responding to a child's communication attempts are very important to her sense of security and worth. In the home environment, language plays the same important role. What happens to families who rarely talk and share? Family members isolate themselves and relationships fall apart, or never take root in the first place. A child who feels that what she has to say is void of worth will also feel that she, herself, is void of worth. Positive, warm interaction is the key to successful communication and a child's sense of worth in the world. And this is a deserving area of a child's daily care that is often overlooked.

CHAPTER EIGHT

Growth Spurt

19–21 Months

At 18 months, your toddler's expressive speech may consist of 10–20 words. However, by the time he is two, he may be using 200! This is quite a growth spurt. From 19–24 months, your child is making dramatic advancements in his language development, not only in his use of new words, but in his understanding of concepts as well.

Labeling (or naming) is fun for the 19-month-old. He enjoys pointing to pictures in books, naming pictures, or asking mother for a name. He's beginning to form categories of objects in his mind, and develops favorites from time to time. When he learns the word for dump truck, he's alert to spot them everywhere—in books, on TV, and on the road.

Earlier, your child was able to understand many words based upon the context of the familiar routines he was engaged in every day. But now, words and phrases do not always have to be supported by environmental clues in order for him to understand. He understands the phrase, "Let's comb your hair" when there is no comb in sight. When you say, "Let's go to McDonald's," he runs and gets his coat. Familiar people do not have to be present in order for him to remember and understand who you are talking about in your conversations. He is now relying less on gestures, facial expressions, and body movements and more on actual words in obtaining useful information about the world.

Your child's speech may now be described as "telegraphic" (after a telegram), predominated by two-word phrases, such as "more milk," "want cookie," and "Daddy car." One phrase may mean many different things, depending on the context or situation at hand. When he says "Daddy car" while pointing to the garage, he may mean, "Daddy's car is in the garage." When he says "Daddy car" while pulling on Dad's pants with his coat under his arm, he may mean, "Let's go for a ride." Accept what your toddler has to say and guess at the meaning if you're not sure. Your encouragement and acceptance will go a long way in building his confidence as he strives to make his needs and wants understood.

Understand your child's willfullness during this stage of development. Your toddler will constantly be testing you, himself, and everything in the environment. He seems to be growing in many ways all at the same time, wanting to achieve everything at once. In trying, though, he will often fail because he is not yet ready to accomplish everything he tries. You can help your child succeed part of the time by being tolerant with his efforts, guiding him when necessary, and making sure his play area is safe.

Developmental Milestones

Understanding and Talking

- Has an expanding, receptive vocabulary of over 100 words, including the names of food, items of clothing, body parts, and the names of people and common objects
- Can carry out two sets of directions, such as "get the ball" and "give it to Daddy"
- Enjoys the narratives of familiar story books read to him

- Understands descriptive words such as "hot," "pretty," and "dirty"
- Understands 10 verbs such as "sit," "look," "eat," "sleep," "open," "close," "get," "walk," and so on
- Refers to self by name
- May make verbal requests ("more milk")
- Begins naming objects upon seeing them, and may frequently ask, "What's that?"
- Uses social greetings more frequently and spontaneously
- In expressive speech, uses 10–20 words or more
- May use some colloquial speech such as, "oh boy," "oh wow," and "all done"
- Tries to imitate phrases and short sentences, often repeating the last word said to him

Motor Skills

- Walks sideways without holding onto furniture
- Pulls a wheeled toy while walking
- Kicks a large ball forward
- Running is smoother and more coordinated
- Gets in and out of a small chair without help
- Throws a ball overhead in a forward direction
- Can push a chair or large box around the room

Toy Play

- Enjoys stacking blocks
- Opens and closes boxes, jars, and other containers
- Matches toys according to physical characteristics (puts blue and red blocks in separate piles when shown)
- Learns through trial and error to put shapes (circle, square, and triangle) in the right hole on a puzzle or form board

- Acts out familiar everyday experiences (eating from spoon, brushing doll's hair)
- Can work simple wooden puzzles with knobs that help when lifting pieces in and out
- Enjoys peg boards, a jack-in-the-box, toys with screwing action, bathtub activity center, picture books, and touch-me (tactile) books

Playtime Activities

Flour Play

Dump several cups of flour into a large bowl or cardboard box and place it on the kitchen floor. Allow your child to explore the flour up to his elbows!

Give him small cups and spoons for dumping, scooping,

Dumping and pouring with flour.

and pouring. Talk about what this experience feels like: "The flour is so fluffy. It feels so soft." For some variation, use other materials such as sand, cornmeal, oatmeal, or crispy rice cereal.

Children learn a great deal about their environment through the sense of touch. To further help your child develop tactile skills, give him many different materials to touch, taste, feel, and play with. Talking about the materials as he is engaged in the activity introduces him to new words that describe the way various textures feel.

Make a Train

This is a fun activity to keep the children occupied when you wash the kitchen floor. Remove the chairs around your kitchen table and assemble them front to back in a long, straight

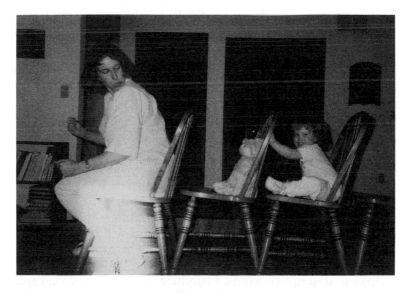

All aboard!

line. You will be the engineer to get the ball rolling. Sit in the front chair and say, "Let's ride the train. Choo choo, chug-a-chug-chug. The train goes fast. Sometimes it goes slow. All aboard!" Use gestures in your pretend play, waving passengers aboard and "steering" the train in different directions.

Your child may attempt to copy parts of the scene, using gestures and imitating words. Or, he may take it all in quietly and play the scene at a later time. At this point, your toddler is more of an imitator than a pretender. He simply copies your actions, but, with time, will come to understand the entire scene of train play. If he has seen pictures of trains in books, plays with toy trains, or has seen them on Sesame Street, he will understand that people ride in trains and then transfer that information to his play.

Later, at the two-year age level, his play episodes will become longer and more props will be used. As his play themes expand, so do his language skills.

Paper Megaphones

Make paper megaphones by rolling 8½ × 11 sheets of paper into cones or cylindrical shapes and taping the ends. Sit on the floor with your child and demonstrate loud and soft sounds. Say, "I can make loud sounds like this . . . and I can make soft sounds like this . . ."

Use your voice differently when you describe what loud and soft sounds are. When you talk loudly, use a deep-pitched voice. When speaking softly, use a light, airy voice. When your child uses a loud voice, cover your ears with your hands and exclaim, "Oh my, that's loud!" Using gestures and animated facial expressions in response to your child will help carry the meaning of the words as well as add enjoyment to the activity.

Each day, so many opportunities arise to introduce your toddler to descriptive words. Introduce the contrast of loud and soft sounds when the occasion arises at home: turning on the

Listen up, everyone!

dishwasher, listening to the hum of the refrigerator, and adjusting the volume on a television set.

Kick Ball

The active 20-month-old is a ball of physical energy—walking, running, and climbing anything of some height. It is especially important to supervise and provide safe climbing situations for your toddler; without a sense of danger or distance, he is apt to try anything.

Help your toddler curb some of this physical energy by playing kick ball. He can now stand on both feet and kick the ball without stepping on it. Use a large, light beach ball so that just a tap from his foot will send it rolling.

Describe your activity. Say, "Justin, kick the ball. Kick the ball to me." Demonstrate for him at first, if necessary. Kick the ball back and forth taking turns. Provide variations by kicking smaller balls into a large container (a basket or a box) turned on its side.

All Fall Down!

Now that your child is able to walk sideways (without crossing his feet), invite him to participate in a game of "Ring around the Rosey." Involve all family members in the game. Hold hands, walk in a circle, and sing the song slowly. When singing, "We all fall down!" raise baby's hands up and down rhythmically so he learns to anticipate what comes next. Meet his gaze so that he can watch your mouth and facial expressions as you sing.

This game is a sure-fire favorite among all children. It mixes movement with song and the anticipation of everyone (even the adults!) falling to the floor. Your toddler will quickly learn when this is about to happen, and may imitate the last word "down," overreacting for the sheer joy of it. Play the game several times, the last time omitting the word "down," and let your toddler fill in the blank. Be prepared; he may request this game often in the future!

Feely Feet and Hands

The mobile toddler loves outdoor play. Introduce him to the various textured objects found outdoors (with your supervision). Let him feel sand and grass on the bottom of his feet. Encourage his exploration by walking on small stones or a warm sidewalk. Let him feel crunchy leaves in the fall and go barefoot in mud puddles in the spring. Talk to him about how each texture feels, using descriptive words, such as smooth, rough, cold, wet, soft, warm, and tickly.

Squishy sand under my feet.

Outdoor sand and water play will be enjoyed by your toddler for many months to come. Fill a plastic tub with water or sand and provide an array of utensils: scoops, spoons, a sifter and sieve, pie pans, funnels, and containers of various sizes.

Cars and Trucks

Children learn to play imaginatively through imitating the behavior of others. At first, your child may copy you moving a toy car along the floor and making the motor sound. Once he associates the label "car" for the real thing, he then can put meaning into his pretend play. Riding in cars may become exciting for him, and he is apt to ask you the names of vehicles if it peaks his interest.

Play on the floor with your toddler and provide an assortment of toy cars and trucks. Move them across the floor, making motor sounds and talking about your activity: "Vroom, vroom, my car goes fast. Let's go fast. I'll follow you. Where are we going?"

Use whatever props you have available in the home or at day care. Use couch pillows to build an enclosure for the cars, or to serve as ramps. Point out the specific parts on the vehicles: wheels, windows, and doors.

It is best to try and follow your child's lead in play, commenting and making suggestions as you go. Be a playful companion rather than a teacher.

Boxes, Boxes

Don't throw away those old boxes. Toddlers enjoy playing with boxes of all sizes: diaper boxes, shoe boxes, and especially appliance boxes that are big enough to crawl around and hide in.

A large box can become a special place for your toddler. Give him a blanket and pillow to put in his box for a cozy retreat. Put his favorite toys inside and encourage him to climb in and get them. Cut holes on the sides through which he can peek out from the inside.

Have him climb into an old diaper box and pretend that he is driving a car. Or, turn the box over and put it on his head, playing a game of "Where did Justin go?" Also, turn the box over on the floor and hide objects under it for him to find. Let him step, crawl, or jump on top and discover what happens when the box won't hold his weight. He may not need you to provide activities for him to do; he will spontaneously create and experiment as he goes along.

Build on his language and problem-solving skills by describing what you see him do and by challenging his efforts in a lighthearted way. Challenging a baby's efforts is not teaching a new skill. It is simply observing what the child is doing and then "scaffolding" him to the next level by increasing the challenge and making the activity a little more difficult or thought provoking.

Bottle of Raisins

Your toddler now possesses the ability to use his thumb and fingers to pick up small objects, and enjoys carrying two small toys in one hand. Give him the opportunity to practice these new discoveries by playing "Bottle of Raisins."

Provide a small container (a small bottle with a screw top) and a bowl of beans or raisins, and ask him to put the raisins inside the bottle: "Put the raisins in the bottle, Justin. Can you help me? Let's put them all in." He may be able to hold the bottle with one hand and release a raisin into it with the other hand. See if he then tries to dump them out.

Dropping raisins in the bottle.

Attach words to his actions of taking the top off the bottle, putting the raisins in, dumping them out, and eating the raisins! Raisins work well, as children love to eat them. However, beans make more noise when dropped, and a bottle of beans is fun to shake. (Supervise when using small objects.)

Often during a fine-motor activity such as this, children are very quiet as they concentrate on the task at hand. It's no wonder; manipulating raisins in and out of a small container can be very challenging for a child! Let him play with containers and objects of various shapes and sizes for further exploration.

Chase Me!

Playing an interactive game with your child provides pleasure and a sense of togetherness for both of you. At this stage of development, the toddler's physical prowess takes preference over other areas, and games of chase are an all-time favorite.

Prepare him for the game by telling him what you are going to do. (Don't frighten or startle without warning or he may be wary the next time.) "Justin, I'm gonna get you. Here I come. I'm gonna get you." Encourage him to get away, and then go after him, exclaiming "gotcha" and rolling around the floor when he's caught. Soon he will understand the game just by hearing the words, and will take off, running with excitement. He may look like he's trying to go faster than his little body will carry him.

Watch out for those corners! Your toddler can run pretty well (albeit, stiffly) and stop on a dime, but he is not quite ready to turn corners smoothly. Tone down your approach if he gets too excited. Coordinating his trunk, legs, and arms smoothly takes time, and he will take many falls in the process.

For variation, switch roles and encourage him to chase you. While he's watching, duck around a corner and say, "Come here Justin; come catch me."

Chasing and catching games continue to be enjoyed by children in many different forms for years to come. Everything from "Duck, Duck, Goose" to a game of tag provide valuable interaction among children and adults.

Activities in Your Daily Routines of Dressing, Feeding, and Bathing Your Toddler

Where Are My Clothes?

Test your child's ability to follow lengthier directions and gather clothing that is out of sight by playing "Where Are My Clothes." Ask him to find two items of clothing and bring them to you.

To the tune of "Are You Sleeping?" sing, "Shoes and socks, shoes and socks, where [gesture] are they? Where [gesture] are they? Get your shoes and socks. Get your shoes and socks. Thank you, Justin. Thank you, Justin."

Mix up items that don't necessarily go together like socks and hat, and pants and mittens. You are challenging your toddler to remember both items and search them out in his room independently. You may be surprised to see that he knows exactly where all his clothing items are kept, if given the chance and the challenge.

Feeding "Baby"

Pretend play with toddlers is a wonderful way to expand their imagination and build on their language skills. Especially popular with young children is the food theme. In the first year, children pretend to feed themselves and their dolls. Into the second year, their theme expands and they become interested in the preparation and serving of food (making cookies out of play-dough, putting them on plates, and passing them around to the guests).

Time for baby's bottle.

While your toddler is seated in his highchair, place an empty cup, bowl, and spoon on his tray. Then place his teddy bear or baby doll on the tray and ask him to "feed the baby." Model the scene for him by giving the "baby" a drink and talking (in an animated, high-pitched voice) about what you are doing. For example, say, "Time to feed baby. My, you look hungry. Would you like some juice?" (Pretend to feed the baby from the cup.) "Here's your applesauce. Yumm, that's good!" (Feed "baby" with the spoon.)

Then, remove your attention and go about your duties in the kitchen, inadvertently observing your child's play. See if he imitates your actions and/or talks to the doll as he plays. Children enjoy copying familiar events as a way of understanding their world better and meeting the social needs inherent in their everyday lives.

Wash My Hands

Help your child learn to wash his hands with your assistance. By listening to your descriptions as you walk through the hand-washing activity, he learns the sequence of behaviors.

Provide a stool so that your youngster can reach the bathroom sink comfortably. Small stepstools will be handy for several years as your child learns to use the bathroom sink and kitchen counter space. Show him how you run the water to fill the sink. Point out the hot and cold faucets, letting him feel the difference, but prepare the water for him until he gets a little older. Let him push the soap pump on liquid soap, or use small novelty hand soaps that will fit in his hand.

Emphasize the order of the activity as he is experiencing it: "First, roll up your sleeves. Next, let's turn on the water. Cold

Learning to wash my hands.

and hot make warm water. Does that feel OK? Now, get the soap. Wash your hands, around and around. Good! Now let's dry. What do we need to dry our hands?" Keep a small hand towel handy and within his reach.

Empty and Full

During bathtime, give your toddler several plastic cups of various sizes. Let him explore the cups and show him how to scoop water into one cup and pour it into another cup. (He may need your assistance pouring from one container into another.) If he needs to use two hands to hold onto the cup, have him pour water into a cup that you are holding. Say, "Look Justin, my cup is empty. Pour some water into my cup, please."

Although at first unsteady, assist him in filling your cup and say, "Now my cup is *full*. My cup is *full*, and your cup is *empty*." He will soon understand the concept of empty and full and may try to imitate the words after you. Remember to talk about empty and full when you are filling his cup with milk at mealtimes as well.

Stimulation Techniques

Your toddler is so eager to learn the names of things around him that a frequently asked question at this stage of development, "What's that?" is often articulated as, "Was dat?" Do not be too concerned about his pronunciation of words at this point. Speech sounds develop in a progressive, orderly fashion with particular sounds appearing earlier and more frequently than others. The sequence of speech sounds development is highly variable from child to child and leaves ample room for individual differences.

At 19 months, a perfectly normal child may mispronounce 50 percent or more of his speech sounds. Consonants will be omitted or substituted for other consonant sounds. For example, your child may say "wabbit" for "rabbit," "yamp" for "lamp," and "an ma" for "grandma." Or, he may reduplicate sounds, producing all the syllables of a word in the same way; "water" may be pronounced like "wa wa" or "bottle" may sound like "ba ba." Sometimes the child's name for something doesn't sound anything at all like the word. For example, one child produced "baby" as "dudu," but he never wavered in his meaning; "dudu" *always* meant "baby."

At this point, accept your child's speech as it is and make a habit of repeating the words accurately after him so that he can hear the corrected form of the word. Children master the pronunciation of words in graduated steps. What is most important at this stage is that your child feels free and relaxed in expressing his needs and desires. It's best to focus on *what* your child is attempting to communicate, rather than *how* he makes the sounds.

CHAPTER NINE

Saying "No!"

22–24 Months

As your child progresses through the age of two, it is not uncommon to experience periods of disequilibrium labeled by our culture as the "terrible twos." During this time, it may seem that much of your talk with your two-year-old is "control talk" ("get down," "no," "don't touch," "stop that").

The amount of control talk can be decreased by thinking ahead and arranging your home so that breakable and potentially harmful objects are not within your child's reach. It may also be helpful to examine your conversational style to see just how often you are giving orders and the tone of voice you use to convey them.

Think of replacing negative statements with concrete and firm statements about what you want your child to do. For example, if your child throws her cup on the floor, instead of shouting, "No, don't do that," you can firmly say, "Cups are not for throwing; cups are for drinking. Keep your cup on the tray, please," and demonstrate by putting the cup back where it belongs. Don't expect instantaneous results. Repetition is the key to learning limits, and your child will test her ability to stretch them at every turn.

When using "no" to deny a request from your child, try to

do so in a respectful tone. Give her a simple reason for your denial, and then close the conversation if she keeps whining. This type of interaction takes a great deal of patience and repetition on your part, but opens the door for richer conversations with your child as she matures. Nothing puts up a barrier to communication more than continual "no's" delivered in a condemning tone of voice.

Your two-year-old has her own way of saying "no" to you as well. Many children at this age show their refusal by simply ignoring a request altogether and pretending they didn't hear it! Or, using their emotions, some children whine, cry, or cling to the caregiver in attempts to avoid accepting an inevitable situation (for instance, being buckled up in a car seat). This behavior may carry on well into the 2½- to 3-year age range, as kids test out their abilities and willfullness in the world.

A two-year-old's contradictory behaviors are sure signs of progress toward growth and independence. All parents go through this stage with their toddlers, bewildering as it may be. Often your child may say "no" to things she wants to do or have, appearing not to completely understand the difference between yes and no. When mother asked, "Sarah, would you like some ice cream?" Sarah immediately responded with an emphatic "no" and then started whining and crying when mother put the carton back into the freezer. Sarah is aware that a question requires an answer; she just hasn't yet made a clear distinction between the *use* of the two replies, or, perhaps, is simply exercising her feelings of control and autonomy. A caregiver can help in these situations by restating the question: "Sarah, would you like some ice cream? Yes or no?" and modeling the correct response for her.

Although now it may feel as though your conversations are somewhat one-sided, with you asking the questions and often even answering them, in another year, conversations with your child will turn into more authentic give-and-take exchanges, with both of you having a more qualitative effect on each other's behavior.

Developmental Milestones

Understanding and Talking

- Understands and responds to simple questions such as "Where's the _____?" or "What's that?"
- Understands 200–300 words
- Understands directions with prepositions, such as, "Put this *on* the table," and "Put this *under* the table"
- Speaking vocabulary is 20–200 words (this varies greatly from child to child)
- Jargon speech begins to drop out
- Answers the question, "What's your name?" with correct first name
- Uses "telegraphic" speech, which consists of two-word combinations to express an idea ("Mommy, sock")
- Uses "no" in refusal ("no night-night," meaning I don't want to go to bed)
- Can imitate two- and three-word sentences
- Relies less on gestures and more on words to communicate

Motor Skills

- Jumps off floor with both feet
- Jumps down from the bottom step
- Can ride a small three-wheeler toy (propels forward with feet)
- Can balance on one foot for a moment or two
- Can go up and down stairs alone, holding onto railing, with both feet to a stair

Toy Play

- Operates toys: winds up music box, puts coin in play cash register; pulls string on See 'n Say

- Copies vertical and horizontal lines on paper with a crayon
- Can stack three or more blocks
- Is aware of size and space—can nest four cups or boxes (putting one inside the other according to size)
- Enjoys creating with clay or playdough, and loves sand and water play
- "Pretends" one toy is another in play: pushes a block like a car, making the motor sound; pretends to wash a doll's face with a towel, then uses the towel as a blanket
- Throws and retrieves objects
- Enjoys rough-and-tumble, active play
- Enjoys hand puppets, stuffed animals, musical instruments, tub toys, balls of all sizes, ride-on toys, hammering toys, and push toys that resemble adult equipment (lawnmower, shopping cart)

Playtime Activities

"I Forgot" Game

Throughout the day, pretend that you forgot to complete a task with your child so that she must initiate communication with you in order to complete it. She will be completely delighted with this fun game, and you are helping her to gain confidence in manipulating her environment. Some examples of "forgetting" are:

- Giving her a bowl of cereal, without a spoon
- Placing her favorite toy on a top shelf, out of reach but not out of sight
- Giving her an empty cup at dinner time
- Providing only one sock when she is dressing

Observe what she does to bring the situation to your attention. Does she point to the desired object, or use words to tell you what she wants? Make it funny by exclaiming, "Oh, silly me. I forgot your _____." Once she catches on to your humor, she will make it a point to keep you straight from then on.

Building Blocks

As children learn to walk and talk, they learn about the world through their own discovery and experimentation. Blocks are an excellent toy that encourages a child's sense of invention.

Provide your child with an assortment of wooden blocks of various shapes and sizes. As the child chooses among blocks of various sizes, as opposed to blocks that are all the same size, she will be required to make decisions about balance.

As your child builds, comment on what she is making: "Wow, that's a high tower." Play side by side with her, making

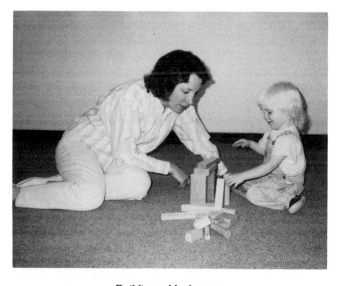

Building a block tower.

your own buildings, and briefly describe what you are making: "This big block will go on top. I hope I can balance it. Uh oh, it fell down!" Make it a relaxed and pleasant atmosphere as you play alongside her, with no pressure on her to converse.

Initially, the child may experiment by stacking the blocks and knocking them down, just to see what happens. She may enjoy building towers, trains, and buildings, imitating you. Or, she may prefer to create her own interesting designs and arrangements without interference from an adult.

By age three, she will use the blocks in dramatic play situations, constructing make-believe settings with houses, roads, and other familiar buildings. A block then becomes a car she can run across the floor, a tower of blocks becomes grandma's house.

Playing with blocks enables your child to explore many spatial concepts (out, into, on top, beside, etc.) as well as symbolically represent features in her real world environment, for example, buildings, cars, and roads.

Blocks are one of your best toy investments. There is no one correct way to use them, and every child uses them in his or her own personal way. *Note:* For younger children, use soft plastic blocks or cloth covered foam cubes.

Bubble Pan

Fill a large pan or bowl with two inches of water and place it on the kitchen floor to use as the bubble pan. Hold one end of a straw up to your child's hand and blow air through it so that she can feel the air pressure on her fingers. Then, show her how to blow air through the straw. Once she understands the idea of blowing, demonstrate blowing bubbles in the pan of water.

Add several drops of liquid detergent to the water, and let her create a panful of bubbles. Talk about what she is doing: "You can blow bubbles. They get bigger, and bigger, and *bigger!*

Blowing bubbles in a bowl.

Let's make some *small* bubbles. Let's make *tiny, tiny* bubbles. Up, up, up and away they go."

At first, your child's blowing efforts may be somewhat sloppy. She may not quickly differentiate between sucking and blowing. It will take some time to master control over the two, but once learned, she will be delighted to blow on many other objects. She will quickly learn that blowing a horn produces a sound, blowing on water makes ripples, and blowing in dad's ear makes him tickle with laughter. Show her how to blow on hot food, too.

The action of blowing is fun and easy. Baby learns that she is in control, and can make something interesting happen. The party favor expands, bits of tissue flutter away, and Ping-Pong balls roll when she blows on them.

During blowing, your child is practicing lip-rounding

movements, which are important for saying the speech sounds /p/, /b/, and /w/, and getting enough breath behind them. Your child is also exposed to different shape, size, and color comparisons as you share the excitement of bubble-making, providing that you describe these attributes during play.

Ping-Pong Balls

Young children possess a sense of inventiveness that we adults lose as we conform to the many roles and expectations society places upon us.

How many things can you think of to do with a Ping-Pong ball? An adult plays table tennis, whereas a child will try out many different things with it, just to discover what it will do.

Provide your toddler with several Ping-Pong balls and let her experiment. Have other props available to encourage a variety of play episodes. For example, use a piece of wood and a pillow and build an incline to roll down the balls. Or, blow the balls across a table, making it a race to the finish line. Put the balls inside an empty paper towel roll, and watch them roll to the other end—the longer the tube, the better.

Once again, use "self-talk," or briefly describe what is happening as it is happening, to build upon your toddler's language skills as she experiments: "Uh oh, Sarah, where's the ball? Here it comes!" Try to follow her lead and let her direct the play as you copy her actions, making enthusiastic comments and giving suggestions when appropriate.

Ladder Walk

The energetic two-year-old is moving all the time. She can walk forward, backward, and sideways. She can even walk up the stairs alone (with both feet on each step), though she needs

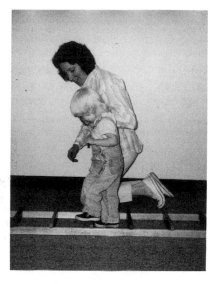

Lift those legs for ladder-walking.

to hold your hand when coming down. She loves to climb anything, jump over obstacles, and throw balls. Any variations on
the subject of locomotion will be a welcome challenge for your
toddler.

Outside, place a ladder on the grass and encourage your
toddler to walk by stepping between the rungs. Hold her hand
at first if she needs assistance: "Pick up your knees. Raise your
knees high, Sarah. Up and over, up and over, over the bar."
Next, pile a couple of old tires under one end of the ladder
(making sure it is securely anchored) and let her experiment
climbing up and down. Guide her foot to the next rung if she
needs assistance. "Sarah's climbing, up and down. Good for
you!"

If your toddler loves to climb, provide safe areas or commercial climbing toys that enable her to practice this skill.

Band Leader

According to the two-year-old, kitchen utensils make wonderful music. Set up a marching band by providing your toddler with the following: a pot and wooden spoon for a drum, a ring of metal measuring spoons for a shaker, and tin pie plates for cymbals. Pass out the instruments to family members or friends as well, and with their help show your child how to march in time with the banging (I mean, music!), and make her the band leader.

Using a chant along with the noise helps to provide direction. Count as you march and describe your activity in a song as you go along: "Marching, marching, marching band. We play music all over the land."

At this point, your toddler is not as interested in sounding out a tune as she is in simply moving her body in time to the music. This kind of sound experimentation is fascinating to the two-year-old, although it may be somewhat taxing on the adult ear.

Collect commercial toy instruments that your child will enjoy for many months to come. A tambourine, harmonica, wooden sticks, maracas, bells, and a triangle all provide interesting musical variations for your toddler.

Bowling

Your toddler has now acquired enough balance to roll a ball while standing. Earlier, she learned to roll and throw while in a sitting position, using both hands. With her increased mobility and coordination, she is ready to aim and roll a ball at a target.

Use a small rubber ball and tall plastic cups (or others that you have available at home/day care). Set the cups upside down in a row about four or five feet away from the starting line. Now, show your toddler how to roll the ball to knock all the cups down. She may begin by throwing overhead, so teach her how

It's a strike . . . almost!

to roll underhand. Also encourage her to bowl until all the cups are knocked down. Assist her in setting up the "pins" for the next person's turn. Emphasize taking turns by saying, "OK Sarah, *your* turn. Good! Now let's set the cups back up. It's *my* turn now." After a few rounds, she will understand the rules of the game.

She is able to take turns when play sequences are kept short, but don't expect her to wait in line for other children. She's too busy and will be distracted into other exploratory play if she has to wait too long. Learning to take turns with many people over a longer period of time continues to develop through age five.

Window Watch

During her first year, your child learned the names of things by experiencing actions that were associated with the names. For example, she learned the label "diaper" after many times watching you lay her down, remove her diaper, and put on a new one. The entire sequence of actions associated with diapering and your naming the event each time helped her to learn the word "diaper."

During her second year, she continues to learn words effortlessly, based upon her experience of the contexts in which they occur. She may remember the name of a bus if you show her a picture of a bus, but she will naturally internalize that new knowledge if you give her a toy bus to play with, or point out the school bus as you are driving down the highway. Words are learned, not taught, in the contexts and activities that you share together.

While riding in the car, briefly talk about what you see. Name the school bus and the city bus. She will be able to conceptualize in her mind the differences and similarities, but this will take time. Point out the cement truck and the taxi cab, and briefly talk about each one: "Look, there's a cement truck. The worker uses cement to make sidewalks." Be brief. As these experiences are replayed, she increasingly becomes aware of their differentiations.

When she points to new and interesting objects, name them for her and give a brief definition. Window-watch at home, naming the actions and sights just outside your front door. Or go window shopping!

Doll Play

Playing mama or daddy is one of the most popular roles children assume in their pretend play. Children are naturally

Fixing lunch for the girls.

inclined to take on the provider role simply because it involves activities that constitute their daily experiences.

Provide props for your child to assume the role of mom or dad. Keep a box of old dress-up clothes handy as props: old shoes, scarves, hats, beads, and belts. She will enjoy dressing up and pretending to take care of her dolls or stuffed animals. Provide props to use with her dolls, such as a table setting, a pillow and blanket, toy bottles, and a hair brush. She will imitate her everyday experiences by feeding the doll, changing its diaper, and putting it to bed.

Your child may enjoy the "actor" role and "talk" her way through the play sequence. Through her verbalizations, she is using language to order the sequence of events in her mind as she plays: "Nighttime, baby. Bottle's all gone. Time for bed." These activities mirror what she sees in real life, and her ability to act them out gives her a sense of order and feelings of self-worth.

Earth and Sky

Observe and learn! Take your child out for a walk and give her a collection bag. Collect seeds, berries, twigs, and rocks. Feel and talk about the different colors, shapes, sizes, and weights of different objects. Call the trees by name: spruce, birch, and cottonwood. Talk about how trees lose their leaves in the fall and blossom in the spring. Talk about what the sun does for us. Look at cloud formations in the sky and talk about what they look like.

It is not necessary to lecture to your child; simply talk about what you have found and she will ask questions and seek elaboration in a natural way. The point is to fully sample the outdoor world with your senses and share these experiences with your child.

Activities in Your Daily Routines of Dressing, Feeding, and Bathing Your Toddler

Clothes Off and On

Repeating words often helps children to understand them and incorporate them into their own vocabulary at an earlier age. At bedtime, think of 10 different ways to say the words "off" and "on" while undressing and dressing. "Shirt off! Shoes off. Pants off. Time for P.J.'s. P.J. pants on! P.J. shirt on. All done!" Children at this age love simple rituals, and will eventually repeat the phrases without any prompting from the caregiver.

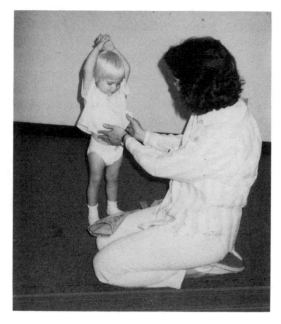

Helping with my shirt.

Using a Fork

Because your child wants to eat the way grown-ups do, introduce a small blunt fork at your next meal. Cut up a few nutritious snack foods (cheese, banana, cooked potatoes) into bite-sized pieces and let her practice spearing the food and putting it into her mouth. She'll be a bit clumsy at first, but tell her what a good job she is doing, anyway. Say, "You're using a fork. Now you can use a spoon *and* a fork, just like Mom and Dad. What a big girl you are!"

Your child's first opportunity to use a fork will be quite interesting for her. She will enjoy the action of spearing the food more than eating it! Some children concentrate very hard on this

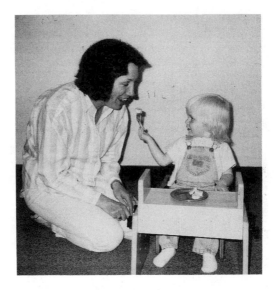

Have a bite, Mom!

activity, repeatedly spearing pieces of food and removing them just for the pure pleasure of accomplishment. Give her a child-sized fork and small balls of playdough for her to pretend feeding her dolls.

Sink or Float

Help your child to differentiate the qualities that make objects float or sink in the bathtub. Although she will notice the differences and experiment on her own, match her actions with descriptions: "Look, your boat stays on top of the water. It floats. Let's try the spoon. Will the spoon float? No, it sinks to the bottom."

Gather objects from both categories and ask your child what she thinks will happen to each one when placed in the water. Let her test it out on her own. Don't bombard her with questions; pause between your statements and observe her reactions to guide you on what to say next. Talk about the properties of her tub toys, washcloth, and soap.

Wipe the Table

Most children, at one time or another, will play with their food and make a mess. This is typical behavior, as your toddler is curious and exploratory with everything else. Therefore, why not food? It is important to set limits, however. It is one thing to dip fingers into a cup of milk, and quite another to fling food at the walls!

After each meal, ask your child to clean up after herself. First, ask her to hand you her cup, dish, and spoon (one at a time). Then say, "Sarah, it's time to clean up. Here's the sponge. Can you wipe your tray?" Let her wipe the tray, but don't expect it to be clean! Praise her, anyway, and give her encouragement. Make her feel good about helping herself.

Give her a warm washcloth and ask her to wipe her face and hands. You may see this same behavior acted out on her dolls during play. A child will imitate the actions and verbalizations in her everyday life in pretend play, perhaps even mirroring mother's directions ("Wipe face, dolly"). This play-acting is not merely imitation, but a true representation of those events which are meaningful in your child's daily life.

Stimulation Techniques

From this point on, your child's understanding of language will be evidenced through her acquisition of more and more specific ideas. She understands many more categories of words and is expanding her observations to more objects, people, and places outside of the home or day care.

Many different meanings can be translated using the same few words based on how your toddler uses the words and the context in which she uses them. It is fascinating to note how many different types of intentions she is able to communicate using the same two- and three-word phrases. Consider the following example. Sarah, seeing the familiar garbage truck, points to it and says, "garbage truck," simply naming what she sees. Later in the day, she sees a garbage can on the neighbor's front lawn and says, "garbage truck?" associating the truck and the can, and questioning where the truck is (hasn't it come yet?) On yet another occasion, she sees a truck that looks similar to the one she knows, and inquires, "garbage truck?" this time to obtain confirmation from you that it matches the one familiar to her.

But soon the specificity of her messages will increase. After using a variety of one- and two-word messages, your child progresses to lengthier utterances, systematically building on her grammatical repertoire and ability to describe events. She can use verbs to name actions, such as "Mama, car go" (meaning, "Look at that car go, mom"). She understands and can talk about possession, as in, "That Daddy chair" (meaning, "That is Daddy's chair"). She is beginning to describe objects: "Pretty doll, mine" (meaning, "My doll is pretty").

Some children skip this short phrase stage and go directly from single words to three- and four-word sentences. It is through your conversations, and not instruction, that your child learns to order words in sentences and create sentences of her own, as well as imitating adult speech.

Most of your child's comments and conversation are rooted in the present moment. She rarely talks about things that are in the future or past, although most two-year-olds remember past events (for example, asking, "Go swimming today?" remembering her trip to the pool yesterday). The two-year-old comments on what she can see, hear, taste, feel, and smell at the moment, which brings about a great deal of fascination for her. Even the stories she likes to hear describe events that she has participated in or watched others carry out. Stories that describe familiar events like playing with dolls, feeding the cat, or brushing her teeth are thoroughly enjoyed at this age.

Things will change quickly in the next six months, however. Your child will begin to understand glimpses of the past and future sequence of events in her life. Words like "pretty soon," "in a minute," "later," "yesterday," and "tomorrow" will gradually become meaningful explanations of what happened during her daily routines.

As your child's language skills become more and more specific, she is able to exert more influence on the objects and people in her environment. She can name, direct, comment, pretend, and share immediate experiences. Her list of adjectives is longer. Whereas earlier she communicated by crying or yelling when unable to open a drawer, she now uses words and phrases ("Help mom, open mom"). By the time she reaches three, she will have learned all that's required to speak in full sentences.

CHAPTER TEN

Listen and Learn
25–27 Months

Listening is an important skill in your child's learning of language. The two-year-old's listening skills are still immature, as you well know by observing how often he is distracted. You must keep your directions and stories short and to the point, lest something else interesting stirs his attention.

Good listening skills do not just appear. As in talking, listening is a progressively learned skill that ripens and grows with maturity. At one year of age, babies recognize the names of familiar people, foods, and toys. By 1½, they respond to and understand complete sentences. Between two and three, your child comprehends short stories and explanations that far exceed his ability to put those same stories into words.

The energetic two-year-old is an active learner who is interested in everything. Notice how you get your child's attention when giving directions. Besides calling his name, it is often necessary to be physically close. You may hold his arms at his side while talking, tap his shoulder, and make sure you get eye contact before asking him to carry out a direction. You may also want to squat down so that you are at your child's eye level and he can easily look directly at you. Give him equal time and opportunity to talk as well. This is a respectful way to teach young children how to listen, and works far better than yelling or repeating yourself with your back turned to him (not showing very attentive listening skills yourself).

To maintain your child's attention, keep your facial expressions interesting and make your speech worth listening to. While reading a book, for example, vary your voice by whispering on the soft parts, becoming louder on the scary parts, and expressing surprise and suspense when appropriate. Make use of the exclamation points and question marks, and change your voice to fit the different personalities of the characters.

Sometimes it will be necessary for you to distract your child in order to gain his attention. For example, when transitioning him from one activity to the next in your daily routine, use chants and rhymes as a distraction, making them up as you go along. If your child withdraws his attention and whines when it is time for you to assist in brushing his teeth, make up a quick short story about the baby walrus who loved pink toothpaste! This immediately draws his attention to you, and you can give him new information in a fun way.

Whispering together, making up stories, listening to music, reading aloud, and drawing your child's attention to sounds around you are all ways to practice listening skills. Children learn how to listen, just as they learn to talk. Caregivers who are interested and attentive listeners will automatically teach their children how to listen well.

Developmental Milestones

Understanding and Talking

- Understands approximately 400 words
- Understands the number concept "one"
- Responds to the question, "What _____ doing?" as in "What's Mommy doing?" or "What are you doing?"
- Understands and responds to two directions involving two

associated objects, as in, "Get your shoes and socks," "Give me your spoon and cup"
- Understands "same" and can match similar objects
- Uses a speaking vocabulary of 50–100 words or more
- Answers questions with a "yes" or "no" reply (though not always appropriately)
- Expresses possession ("Daddy's car")
- Talks in two- and three-word phrases (or more) most of the time
- Uses the words "in," "on," and "under" to indicate where something is located
- Can identify actions in pictures and recognize what happens next in familiar stories
- Uses pronouns (I, me, mine, you) in his speech
- Is beginning to use plurals ("Mommy, see dogs")
- Can pronounce many consonant sounds correctly (p, b, w, m, n, h, t, d, ng, k, and g)

Motor Skills

- Climbs up a ladder and slides down on a small slide
- Stands on tiptoes
- Holds arms out to catch a large ball
- Can run while carrying a toy under his arm
- Jumps down from a small step
- Is learning how to ride a tricycle
- Makes large circular movements with crayon on paper

Toy Play

- Play sequences become longer—for example, puts blocks in a trailer, hooks trailer up to truck, and drives, making a motor sound

- Uses more language during toy play: pretends to drink from an empty cup and says, "more juice"
- Can string three beads
- Puts several blocks in a row to make a train
- Likes looking at books and turns pages
- Puts toys away in toy box when asked
- Enjoys construction toys, simple puzzles, balls, feely grab bags or boxes, shape sorters, nesting toys, string beads, dolls with accessories, small hand puppets, peg boards, and colored cubes

Playtime Activities

Poetry Reading

Poetry and rhyme stimulate the imagination, are very enjoyable to listen to, and give your child the rhythmic sense of language.

There are many children's poetry and rhyme books that can be checked out of the library, or you can make up your own verses using the child's name and repeating words frequently in the phrase. For example:

> There was a little boy
> Who gave me lots of joy
> His name is Justin B.
> Silly Justin B.
>
> He claps, he sings, he runs
> He twirls and flops and kicks
> Silly Justin B.
> And his silly little tricks

Recommended poetry books include:

- *My little book of poems.* A Golden Book. Western Publishing Co., Inc., 1983.

- *A bug in a jug and other funny rhymes,* by Gloria Patrick. Scholastic Book Services, 1970.
- *A child's garden of verses,* by Robert Louis Stevenson. Random House, 1978.
- *Where the sidewalk ends,* by Shel Silverstein. Harper & Row, 1974.

Whisper to Me

Children find whispering a very special way to talk. It is amusing to them because it is so private and different from normal talking.

Put your finger to your lips and say, "Sh . . . let's whisper." Talk in a whisper while telling your child a secret. Encourage

"What? I can't hear you!"

him to tell you a secret using a special whisper voice. Tell him how it tickles your ear when he whispers to you.

Changing the way you talk will keep your toddler interested and teach him how to control and change his voice at will. He will also be required to listen most intently to the message.

What's That Sound?

Pay attention to environmental sounds around you and take the opportunity to point them out to your toddler. Just by asking, "Did you hear that sound? What's that sound?" he will be alerted to the many different sounds around him every day.

See if he can identify and match sounds to their sources. Turn off the TV or radio. Walk around the house together, pick out a sound to identify, and ask, "Can you hear the refrigerator humming?" Walk him closer to the sound, drawing his attention to it. The house will need to be fairly quiet so that he is able to discriminate and pick out different sounds. This takes attention and concentration.

Examples of sounds to identify include: people sounds–coughing, sneezing, whistling, clapping hands, baby crying; indoor sounds–running the dishwasher, doorbell and phone ringing, glass breaking, a dropped dish, toilet flushing, slamming doors; and outdoor sounds–an airplane flying overhead, dogs barking, a road grader, the noises of birds and squirrels, rain falling, sirens, thunder.

Crayon Doodle

To a young child, scribbling is art! Provide your child with large sheets of paper and crayons (younger children can better grasp larger crayons). Stay away from dictating what color to use or what shapes to draw. He is too young to be told to stay in

Drawing time with Mom.

the lines in coloring books as well. Rather, play alongside with your child, making lines and circles that he can imitate if he chooses. If your child is given many opportunities to experiment with paper and crayons, you will see more confidence and boldness of strokes in his pictures.

Make large, sweeping, circular movements with your crayon. Say, "Wow, a circle. Round and round and round I go," as you make repetitive circles without lifting your crayon from the paper. Pairing a motor movement (drawing) with a repetitive sound ("round and round and round") provides a rhythm that the child can easily fit into. As he scribbles, you may then hear him imitating the words, and, in this interactive process, he is learning the names of shapes and colors in an inadvertent way.

To make sure your child doesn't scribble on cupboards and walls, supervise his activity closely. Work at the kitchen table and bring the crayons out only when you are ready to spend some time drawing together. Tell your child that you draw on paper only, and that when you are finished, the crayons will be put away. The teaching of the proper use of objects is accomplished very gradually, but this method is far more favorable than not allowing certain activities at all out of fear that household items will get broken or dirty.

Don't forget to hang your child's pictures on the refrigerator (at his eye level) for all to enjoy.

Bubble Chase

Blowing bubbles is an activity that children of all ages enjoy. In fact, adults are equally fascinated with the fun of bubble making.

Bubbles can be purchased in the toy section of most grocery stores. Or, you can make your own using liquid soap, water, and glycerine (obtained at a drug store).

Show your child how to blow the bubbles. Exaggerate your lip movements and slowly blow so that he can see how the bubble is formed. Blow bubbles up high for him to jump and reach for. Blow bubbles down low so he must stoop and bend to pop them. Encourage him to chase the bubbles until they pop or disappear. Describe the actions involved. "Get the bubble, Justin. Get it! Pop, pop! You popped it."

Give your child the opportunity to try blowing bubbles on his own. The dipstick wand sold in bottled bubbles is often difficult for little ones to manipulate. Some bubbles come in containers that the child simply squeezes and the wand pops up fully loaded and ready for blowing. Initially, most children blow a little too hard. Blow gently on your child's arm so he can feel how to blow softly. It takes some experience to regulate the breath flow just right, but once successful, he'll want to practice bubble blowing over and over again.

Always make sure to supervise the bubble activity. When learning to use the wand, children often put their mouths on it

Get those bubbles!

while attempting to blow, and the taste of soap bubbles is not very pleasant (as your child will quickly learn on his own!).

Fly with Wings

The appeal of action games and activities cannot be overstated when playing with a two-year-old. Body movements are somewhat limited compared to older children, but the two-year-old uses his arms and legs in more varied movements than previously seen in the stiff-legged toddler.

So go ahead and fly with wings. Attach streamers of crepe paper to strips of masking tape and tape them along the lengths of your child's arms (your arms, too). Show him how the streamers blow in the breeze as you run around the yard: "Look, Justin, I'm flying like a bird. See my wings. Let's be birds." Flap

Pretending to be a bird.

your "wings" like a bird, make silly bird sounds, demonstrate graceful flowing movements, and topple to the ground with exhaustion.

Sharing physical activities and engaging in pretend play provides good exercise and stimulates the imagination. Make a nest or place to call home out of an old blanket and watch how your child may act out familiar daily experiences through the newly found bird character.

Feely Grab Bag

Everyday, children encounter multiple sensory experiences that inform them about the world. A child learns rough and

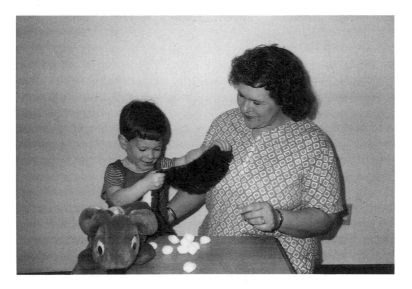

This feels soft and furry.

smooth by feeling the contrast of daddy's unshaven beard and mommy's soft skin; he feels the differences between the smooth skin of a banana and the bumpy texture of an avocado.

Collect objects from around the home or day care and place them in a paper bag. Collect items such as cotton balls, sandpaper, satin, a piece of fur, shells, coins, and marshmallows. Tell your child you are going to play the "feely" game, as you take turns picking something out of the bag and explore it together.

Solicit his interest by turning it into an anticipatory game. Say, "Justin, look. What's in my bag? Shall we look together?" all the while being rather secretive about it. "Your turn first. Take one thing out. Only one." When he pulls an item out, name it and describe how it feels. Use the word "feel" several times so he understands and matches the word with the sensation. "Oh, it's cotton. Feel the cotton. It's so soft." Rub the cotton ball on his cheeks or the back of his hand.

Next, tell him it's your turn, so that he understands that this is a game with back and forth activity. "Oh, I got the quarter. Feel the quarter, Justin. It feels really hard." Tap it on the table a few times, showing him its durability (not its spending power, just its durability!).

Later in the week, draw your child's attention to something hard, soft, rough, or smooth in your everyday activities together. For example, during shopping, say, "My, this melon is hard. Feel this melon, Justin. It's hard. I like to buy softer melons; they taste sweeter."

Jumping Bean

Running and jumping may just be the two-year-old's most favorite pastimes. Too tired to walk? Your child will probably still run. Worried about your bedsprings? The purchase of a rocking horse is a great investment at this stage of development.

There are many ways to give your child additional jumping activities that are safe and can be incorporated into your daily routine. Place a couple of strips of masking tape on the carpet and encourage your youngster to jump over one, then the other. Hold him under the arms, or take his hand if he needs assistance while jumping.

Also, let him jump off of pillows placed on the floor. Show him how to jump in and outside of a circle (made of thin strips of tape). Pretend to be jumping beans! Play some lively exercise music and jump in place, sideways, or backwards: "Jumping beans, jumping beans, Justin and I are jumping beans."

Outside, practice jumping off of curbs and over sidewalk cracks. Pretend to be kangaroos and jump around the yard. Let him jump off of raised surfaces (a few inches high), but make sure a soft landing is provided.

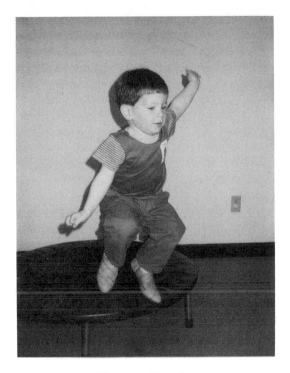

The joys of jumping.

Rubbing Noses

Many families share gestures and jingles that are special and familiar only to them. These special games grow out of everyday interactions together and become a way to amuse each other, as well as smooth over the many emotional upheavals toddlers experience on a daily basis.

Give your toddler lots of snuggles and hugs. Rub noses for the fun of it, bounce him on your knee, and tune into his world for a few moments before he races off to his next exploration. He

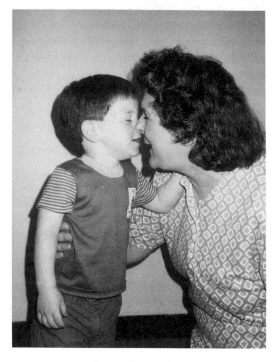

It's nice being close.

depends on these fleeting, yet secure, moments with a care-giver, someone to briefly "touch in" with him from time to time as he plays and explores in his surroundings.

These interactive gestures are a special way of communicating with your child. A silly word you both share, a special wink from dad, a distinctive gesture (like rubbing noses or pats on the head) shared by close friends and family are all ways to foster genuine interaction with your child. Some parents use funny words or rhymes as terms of endearment: "I love you, my little Skinamarinkado! You're the sweetest little pumpernickel in the whole world! Where's my Tina, ballerina?"

Children learn to trust their caregivers (whether it be mom, dad, or day care), feeling happier and more secure when treated with respect and fun-loving care.

Happy and Sad

For many months, your child has been able to distinguish your mood by hearing the tone of your voice and seeing the expression on your face. You can help him to express himself more clearly in the months ahead by labeling those emotions. This way he learns that he can use words to tell you how he is feeling.

It will take a long time for him to use "feeling" words accurately; he may use one word to mean many things at first. But you are opening the door to better communication, showing him that you trust and support his attempts at telling you how he feels. The entire idea of sharing feelings and using words rather than explosive gestures in communicating is one that we, as part of a society, must be taught and nurtured in childhood.

When sharing happy feelings, label them for him, saying, "Gosh, Justin, you look so happy; you love birthdays, don't you?" When your child sees someone crying, label it for him, without being judgmental. "Yes, Justin, that little boy is sad. It's OK to be sad; sometimes we all are sad." Respect and accept the entire realm of human emotions in your child, without labeling one as better than another.

It is very useful to name emotions for a young child when it is clear he is not able to express his feelings and is trying to gain attention in other ways. When Jamie's dad came home from work, the first thing he would do was sit down and read the paper. The first thing Jamie would do was hit dad repeatedly, annoying him. This was Jamie's way of asking for hugs first. Perhaps dad could acknowledge these feelings by saying, "You are so angry, Jamie. How about a few hugs for Dad?" Dad learns that Jamie is asking for attention by hitting, so he takes the time for greetings and hugs. Jamie gradually learns from dad's example that he can use words ("How about a few hugs?") instead of actions (hitting) to get what he wants.

Learning to express emotions can be a very sophisticated skill for a young child. But as your child hears and sees how problems can be solved and feelings understood by watching other adults, he comes to learn that language, rather than fists and tantrums, may be used to express his feelings.

Other examples of labeling emotions may be when one is annoyed, frustrated, feeling bad, pleased, surprised, hurt, and excited.

Activities in Your Daily Routines of Dressing, Feeding, and Bathing Your Child

Naming Colors

Encourage your child's participation in the process of clothing selection by both of you choosing what he is to wear for the day. Enlist his help in finding the items and opening and closing dresser drawers.

Name the color of each item as you pull it out of the drawer: "Oh, a red shirt. And here's your blue shirt." Give him a choice: "What would you like to wear? Your red shirt or blue shirt?" If he points to one, name it again, saying, "Oh, the red shirt. OK, let's put on your red shirt."

He will need to hear the names of colors many times before he will be able to differentiate them. You are already helping him learn the names by labeling the colors as you make your selection together. Remember to occasionally point out the colors of other objects in your daily routine.

Spoons and Forks

While you are preparing a meal, set your toddler at the table for some practice in sorting similar objects into piles. Provide

"The fork goes in here."

him with several spoons, forks, and two tall plastic cups in which to place the silverware. Hold up a spoon and say, "Let's put all the spoons into this cup," and demonstrate by placing a couple of spoons into one of the cups (one at a time). Then, hold up a fork and say, "Let's put all the forks into this cup," as you place a couple of forks into the second cup. Next, ask him, "Can you do the rest?"

If necessary, assist him in placing each utensil into the proper cup, alternating between spoons and forks, until he gets the idea. Later, increase the variety and number of objects for him to sort.

Other items suitable for sorting include blocks of various sizes and colors, poker chips, beads, and buttons. Let your toddler organize some of your mismatched belongings. Separate your jumbled earrings into pairs, or clean out the hall closet and pair up the hodgepodge of shoes, boots, and gloves.

Motorboat Fun

Provide an assortment of colorful plastic boats of various sizes for your toddler to play with in the bathtub. Emphasize the concepts "fast" and "slow" by pushing the boats on the surface of the water at different speeds and describing your actions.

Say, "Look, my motorboat goes fast," and make the motorboat sound as you glide your boat across the water. Sing the jingle, "Motorboat, motorboat, go so fast. Motorboat, motorboat, step on the gas!" Later, move the boat slowly. Exaggerate slow body movements and slow down your rate of speech. "I'm going slow. Slow motorboat." See if your toddler can differentiate between the two actions, according to your directions. Say, "Can you show me a fast motorboat? Make it go fast. Now show me a slow motorboat. What does a motorboat sound like?"

Dressing and Undressing

Young children are capable of taking care of their needs with guidance and direction from a loving caregiver. Most parents lead busy lives, and may continue to do things for their child that he is capable of doing for himself, rather than taking the time to guide him in the learning process. This behavior is habit-forming, but with some awareness, a parent can easily turn things around and involve the child in the activities of self-care, being mindful, of course, of the child's developmental level and abilities.

The two-year-old is ready to help with undressing skills. Start small and teach your child in graduated steps. It takes time to master a new skill, and it is very frustrating for a child when a parent becomes impatient and finishes a job that the child is diligently trying to complete. If the job is too difficult, break it down into easier steps (like taking the child's shoes off halfway), so that the child can reap the benefits of success.

It is much easier learning to undress than dress, so a good

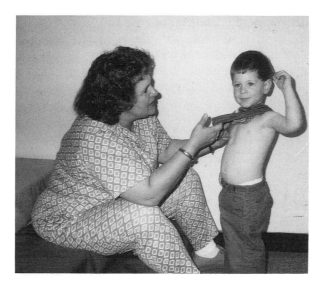

I can help with dressing.

place to start is to help your child learn to take off his shoes, socks, and pants before bedtime. During this ritual, there is a myriad of language vocabulary and concepts that can be built into your activity.

Sit on the floor, next to your child, and show him how to remove his socks. (He's been removing socks for a long time, right? Usually when you'd rather they be kept on.) Describe your actions: "Let's take your socks off. Push down at the ankle like this. Pull on the heel, like this."

Then, while standing, show him how to remove his pants, pushing them down and lifting his legs out one at a time. This is a bit more difficult than removing shoes and socks. Name his body parts in the process: "Let's take your pants off now. Use both hands and push them down. Good! Lift one leg out. OK. Now the other leg. Alright! Let's sit down. Now pull them off. Super!"

Other self-help routines that your toddler is capable of tackling, with your assistance, include washing hands, brushing teeth, wiping up spills, and tasks they have seen a parent perform such as stirring food, dusting furniture, sweeping floors, turning the TV on and off, putting toys away, and, of course, delaying bedtime.

Stimulation Techniques

In conversations with your toddler, it is important to remember that he is a significant participant who deserves respect and attentive listening. Although at times he may become frustrated in trying to communicate his observations to you, listen and think before you react.

As Justin's father tucked him into bed for the night, Justin, with tears in his eyes, sat up and cried, "Daddy, Daddy, I see monster!" Clearly Justin was distressed. There are several ways in which Dad could respond to Justin's feelings: "Don't be silly, there's no such thing as monsters," or "You sound frightened; where's the monster?" The latter response encourages more dialogue between father and son, whereas the former immediately puts a halt to the conversation, and discourages Justin from feeling that what he has to say has worth.

Consider this scenario: A family is enjoying their dinner, when the sound of a jet is heard overhead.

CHILD (excitedly pointing to the ceiling): "Mommy, Mommy."

PARENT: "Settle down, Justin, and eat your meat."

CHILD (waving arms, pointing): "Pane (plane), Mommy, pane!"

PARENT: "Watch it or you'll spill your milk, Justin. Eat your meat, please."

Justin clearly had something significant to say, and his parent did not take the effort or time to figure out what. Listening to your child and providing additional information when appropriate will help him to use language effectively in all situations. Expanding upon what he says adds to the dialogue more information for him to think about. A more thoughtful approach would have been:

CHILD: "Pane (plane), Mommy, pane!"

PARENT: "You hear a plane? Let's go to the window and look."

CHILD: "See pane (plane), Mommy. Wow!"

PARENT: "Yes, it's a big plane, flying very low." (Here, the parent expands or adds information by describing the plane.)

Listening to what your child is trying to communicate and respecting his feelings will take patience and conscious effort on your part. But aren't active listening and mutual respect the kinds of behaviors you would expect from others in your conversations with them? With conscious effort and a little practice, the way in which you respond to your child will soon become automatic.

CHAPTER ELEVEN

Expanded Learning
28–30 Months

At the 2½-year age level, your child's talking skills are much more versatile and specific than they were at 24 months. By now, your toddler may say her full name when asked. She may refer to herself as "me" or "I," whereas six months earlier she used her proper name ("Sarah do it").

Vocabulary has increased dramatically and she can talk in short sentences, often boasting about what she can do ("I fix it") and contradicting herself in the same breath when she needs your help ("Mommy fix it!").

Refusing to do what she is asked to do may be evidenced by a flat "no!" or she may simply ignore you. When she asks "why?" every time you ask her to do something, her questioning may seem to be a way of resisting or stalling, rather than a true request for more information.

Be patient! This expanded learning about the world has captivated your child's full attention. She has a powerful drive to talk, while constantly learning new words and concepts. Her language skills are progressing by leaps and bounds. During her second year, she will already be using almost half of the 500 most frequently used words in typical adult conversations. By the time she is three, her talking vocabulary may well approach the 900-word mark!

Keep in mind the following points that will encourage your child's expanding language skills:

1. Squat down to her level and listen while she talks to you. Try not to dominate the conversation, and ask questions for further elaboration if there is something you don't understand.
2. Pay attention to *what* your child has to say, not *how* she is saying it. Repeat mispronounced words or grammatical blunders if you like, without calling attention to absolute correctness. Talking naturally is not a language lesson, and your child will learn from your example, rather than from your instruction.
3. Respect and encourage times of silence. Talking is not necessary all of the time, and can become empty chatter that is irritating to listen to. There are times when your attempts at conversation will be met with silence. That's OK. We all enjoy quiet times as well as social times, and your child's choice should also be respected.

Developmental Milestones

Understanding and Talking

- Understands most adult sentences
- Understands and carries out two related commands given at one time (will put toys, clothes, shoes, or other objects away when asked)
- Knows many new vocabulary words
- Identifies actions, such as jumping, running, pushing
- Notices fine details in pictures
- Recognizes and names herself, and other familiar people, in photographs
- Understands more descriptive words such as "big," "soft," "heavy," "tall," "pretty," "fast"
- Understands "all" as in "Put all of the forks in the drawer"

- Imitates words and changes speech sounds around to make up her own silly words
- Talks in three- or four-word phrases or short sentences most of the time
- Makes emphatic demands of adults, as in "Tie my shoe"
- May ask "why?" frequently in response to a parental request (often using it to stall rather than obtain more information)
- Can identify objects by their use, by answering questions such as "Show me what you read," "What do you wear on your feet?"
- Uses the words "in," "on," "under," or "beside" to tell where something is located
- Has a speaking vocabulary of 300 or more words
- Asks for help with her personal needs
- Can repeat a sentence 4–5 words in length
- Uses plurals by putting /s/ on the end of words
- Uses pronouns such as "I," "me," "my," "mine," "he," and "she"
- Uses singing patterns in songs such as "Happy Birthday"

Motor Skills

- Can walk a few steps on tiptoes
- Runs and gallops, taking short steps on her toes
- Step-jumps from a stair 18 inches from the floor
- Balances on one foot for a few moments
- Holds pencil or crayon with more mature grasp (between thumb and fingers)
- Snips with scissors

Toy Play

- Engages in dramatic three-step play (for example, arranges dishes on table, feeds herself and doll, puts doll to bed)

- Pretends that the puppet or doll is carrying out an act (puppet washes another puppet's face with washcloth)
- Enjoys lacing-cards, blocks that snap together, cars and trucks, dolls, books, balls, cardboard boxes, small slides, ride-on toys, rhythm instruments, plastic interlocking rings, and large plastic nuts and bolts

Playtime Activities

Puppet Show

An excellent language builder is a puppet show, which can be staged with items you already have around the house or day care. Move your couch away from the wall, and kneel out of view, using the top of the couch as a stage area. Or, lay a card table or a large, empty box on its side and kneel behind it. If you don't have hand puppets, use stuffed animals instead.

The puppets can be used to act out familiar experiences or events that your child can understand or relate to. "I feel sad. I lost my new ball." "Oh, it's OK, I'll help you find it." A puppet can scold, tease, or console another puppet. Make the puppets talk in different voices and color your speech with inflection. Oftentimes, children will say much more about how they feel when they talk "through" a toy or puppet in pretend play. Keep your dialogue short and lively.

Afterward, you be the audience, with your child as the puppeteer. Initially, she may say only a few words and abruptly quit; that's OK. Respond with eager applause. Her play sequences will be short, and she will want to switch roles frequently, or have you both play simultaneously. Follow her lead in the activity.

Puppet play is simple and a great deal of fun, especially with older preschoolers to serve as models for the little ones. Puppet play encourages a child's imagination, and reinforces language practice through listening, imitating, and organizing thoughts into words.

Note: If your child chooses not to participate in the puppet show, don't be coercive or discouraged. Again, many children prefer to watch and listen rather than get directly involved, and this is simply a personality difference. For others, it takes a longer time to warm up to the activity. Rest assured that she is learning by watching and listening, especially if a number of other children are involved.

Shadow Talk

What is a shadow? Point out how we make shadows by standing with our backs to a light source. Explain to your child what a shadow is, and show her how to make shadows on the wall with your hands and fingers.

As a follow-up activity, place a large sheet of newsprint paper on the floor, have your child lie down on the paper, and trace her outline with a crayon. Cut out the figure, and hang it on the wall at her eye level so she can compare herself to her "shadow." Ask her questions about her shadow: "Here is your pretend shadow. Does she look like you? Can your shadow talk? Let's color her clothes. What does she like to eat?" (Do not rattle off questions; give your child plenty of time to respond, then base your next question on her train of thought.)

Children approaching three are capable of more conceptualizing, and enjoy discovering similarities and differences between things. Asking questions and briefly commenting on these contrasts makes for a richer and more varied learning experience.

Grocery Shopping

Although grocery shopping may be a harried time, your child is ripe for all kinds of language learning as she is wheeled down the colorful aisles of the grocery store. The 28-month-old views the shopping excursion as a cornucopia of discoveries.

She is very excited by the colorful displays and whirlwind of people, which may serve to make her even more active.

You can make this chore more interesting rather than hectic by calling your child's attention to the items you need and making her feel a part of the shopping process: "We need cereal. Can you find the Cheerios? Yes, they come in a big, yellow box"; "Let's get some ice cream. What kind shall we choose?"; "What do you like to eat best? Bananas are your favorite? You're just like a monkey! I like pizza. I'll make pizza for dinner tonight."

The same approach can be used if you're accompanied by more than one child, although it will take more time and patience to finish your shopping. In the long run, the payoffs are worth it. Children learn to recognize and name many new items, as well as acquire appropriate behavior in public places, with your guidance.

Finger Painting

Finger paints are available in the toy sections of most grocery stores, or you can even use chocolate pudding on white paper for a yummy mess!

Give your child the opportunity to feel the smoothness of the paint or pudding on her hands, and experiment with the results. This is a fun sensory activity that many children enjoy; however, some children will have no part in getting messy, and don't like the feel of paint squishing through their fingers. Demonstrate first and let her know it's OK to be messy sometimes.

Tape corners of a large sheet of white paper onto her tray. Drop several tablespoons of paint on the paper and guide her hands, letting her poke and squeeze the paint through her fingers. Move her hands in circles, first one hand, then the other, and finally both hands together. Describe your activity: "It feels smooth and soft. Let's make big circles; let's make little circles. Go round and round and round. I can make lines with my fingers."

Or, you may want to approach the activity without direc-

Messy finger painting.

tion. Simply place paint or pudding on the paper and let her touch and experiment on her own, describing her actions and following her lead.

Rock Collection

Children at this age are not interested in collections as a long-lasting activity, but you can introduce the notion of collecting items simply for exploration.

Go outside and explore together. Bring along discarded egg cartons for collecting items of interest. If you live in the city, take a drive to the country, where trees, grasses, and rocks can be explored. Fill your egg carton with stones, twigs, and bugs. Putting them in the carton makes your toddler feel that she has a special place for them, and she can refer to them later, showing them to other family members. Talk to her about what you find

Look what I found!

and name the items, giving a brief description of each one: "Feel this rock, Sarah. It's so smooth. This one feels cold and hard. Wow, you found a rock with spots!"

Small children will be most interested in the here and now, what is happening in the present moment. She may pretend to count the items, drop them in and take them out of the container repeatedly, or feel them once and toss them over her shoulder. But the important thing is that she is observing previously unnoticed details in her world, and learning new vocabulary words to describe them.

Exercising Together

Children need to move around and express their endless reservoir of energy on a daily basis. In places where children receive little outdoor play, indoor exercise can be a life saver.

Exercising can bridge the gap between the differences in age and abilities of mother and child; they can exercise together at their own speed and pace, yet still have in common the benefits and joy of movement.

Many mothers today enjoy aerobic exercise at the end of the work day to relieve stress and stay in shape. Let your child watch your workouts, and encourage her participation. Don't direct any of her movements. Simply watch her imitate your movements of stretching, bending, and running in place. Exercise videos are helpful in getting everyone motivated to follow a specific set of exercises, and kids love the steady beat and energetic rhythm of the music (if it's not too loud).

Besides the physical exercise, there are numerous action words your child will learn in your workouts together: run, jump, stretch up, stretch down, touch your toes, hands over your head, touch the ground, turn around, bend at the waist, to name a few.

Hand Prints

With only a few materials, you can create a "firsthand" experience for your child that she will be proud to show others upon completion. Using washable tempera paint, white paper, and a paint brush, make hand prints.

Paint the child's fingers and palms and show her how to make a print. Make your hand print next to hers, and compare them: "Mommy's hand is big. Sarah's hand is small. When Sarah grows up, her hand will be big as Mommy's." Describe how it feels to have paint brushed on your palm. Talk about the color of the paints you used. Count the fingers on each hand aloud. Let your child experiment by making multiple prints in whichever way she chooses.

Remember to hang the finished product for other family members to observe. Hanging your child's picture gives family members the opportunity to connect with the child's activities during the day, talk to her about them, and establish a common ground with her. This is especially important if she attends a day care, and is away from family members for most of the day.

Snowman

During the winter months, gather up a large bowl of snow and bring it inside for experimentation at the kitchen table. Exploring the properties of snow indoors feels very different than experiencing it in outdoor play.

Tell your child you are going to build a snowman indoors! Using a large cookie sheet, encourage your child to transfer snow from the bowl to the cookie sheet. Let her play with it in whichever way she chooses, perhaps poking her fingers in and scooping out snow with her hands. Talk to her about the sensations. How does it feel? Does it feel cold on her hands? Rub a little snow on her cheeks. Take a taste of the snow. Is it cold like ice cubes?

To make the snowman, make snowballs and place one on top of the other on the cookie sheet. Use raisins for the eyes and mouth. Reserve some snow in the bowl and place it in a sunny window to show her how snow melts into water.

Heavy and Light

How does it feel to carry something heavy? How does it feel to carry something light? A child learns the difference through feeling and, as in learning many other vocabulary words, understands the meaning through multiple experiences with the objects.

Children often learn the most salient of the two words in a contrast, for example, first understanding heavy before light and understanding big before little. They remember that which makes the biggest impression on them.

Ask your child to help with easy everyday chores, for exam-

I can carry **heavy books.**

ple, moving books while you are dusting. Ask her to hold a heavy book or two and say, "Gee, Sarah, that feels heavy. Can you carry all of that? Whew, it's heavy." Give her many experiences of heavy in a natural way during home or day care activities. Let her help carry a heavy (for her!) grocery item, hold a tool (such as dad's hammer), and help push the vacuum cleaner, describing how it feels.

Make a Cave

Encouraging imaginative play in two-year-olds is a wonderful way to foster creative thought and language skills.

Caregivers and older children are often helpful in enticing youngsters into pretend play as they provide good character models and demonstrate varied uses of props. But joining in

"Come see my cave."

isn't necessary. Some caregivers prefer to watch the pretend activities without actively participating; this is fine, too, as everyone's style of interaction differs.

It is important to provide toys and materials that can be played with in a variety of ways. Sometimes elaborate play scenes can be created with simple props.

Collect several of the largest blankets you can find around the home or day care. Set up chairs or stools in a circle, and drape the blankets over the top, creating an enclosure. Now you have a cave, castle, house, jail, or simply a great hiding place. Let your child pick the toys she would like to bring into the cave. Then proceed to follow her lead. Try to be sensitive to your child's level of play, and be careful not to take over or get too elaborate. If she starts to talk about finding a safe hiding place from the monsters outside, stay on her train of thought!

"OK. Everybody come in now. Hurry. The monster's coming."

"Help, Sarah. My foot's stuck in this hole. I can't get it out" [holding leg, mother pretends to be stuck].

"Here, take Timothy [hands mother her stuffed gremlin]. He's real strong. Timothy help you, mom."

Small, enclosed spaces for play are very intriguing to children. Small spaces allow the child to be in control, where she can pretend to be safe from the outside world. Favorite enclosures in the home or day care may include behind furniture, under sinks, draping a blanket over the top of a bunk bed or table, and inside closets.

Activities in Your Daily Routines of Dressing, Feeding, and Bathing Your Child

Sorting Clothes

On laundry day, you can encourage your child's participation by having her help you sort clothes into various piles. Make a pile for each family member. Pull an item out of the laundry basket, and ask, "Whose shirt is this? Yes, this is Dad's shirt. Let's put it in Dad's pile. Whose sock is this? Oh, it's Sarah's. Put it in Sarah's pile." Kids feel quite proud when they can help with simple household chores, and are well aware of what belongs to who in the family.

Cooking Time

Turn the kitchen over to your little helper. While you are in the kitchen preparing a meal, set your youngster up with a food experience that will make her feel capable and have lots of fun.

Helping sort the laundry.

Provide her with a variety of ingredients and utensils: large bowl, spoons, cups, forks, scoops, water, food coloring, flour, salt, and pepper. Let her pretend to make a cake by scooping, dumping, and combining her ingredients in her own way. You will be surprised at her creativity. Ask her what she is making and tell her it looks delicious. Also describe the colors she is working with. Name the utensils and compare concepts: "This water is cold. Oh, you put flour in the water, and then you made it red! I'm making pizza for dinner; what are you making?" She will enjoy this pretend play in which you are not specifically directing her through a real recipe, but, rather, letting her create and pretend on her own.

Wash Your Bellybutton

Let's see how many body parts your youngster can locate as you name them. Give her a washcloth and play this game. Ask her, "Where's your bellybutton?" As she points, then exclaim, "Wash it! Where's your nose? Right. Wash it. Where's your knee? Good, wash it!"

This game usually turns out to be a bit slap happy, especially if you increase the speed of your directions. Try pairing two body parts together and say, "Knees and feet. Eyes and nose. Ears and toes."

Reverse roles and ask her to have you point to various body parts. Sometimes pretend to get it wrong and see if she'll correct you.

Zip My Coat

The nearly three-year-old is ready to zip a zipper up and down, although getting a zipper started will be learned much later when she has more fine motor control. Zippers are so intriguing to little ones that you need not interfere with the unzipping routine. Most children at this age are insistent upon doing it themselves, and are proud to demonstrate their newest accomplishment. If assistance is needed, hold the coat material tightly, making it easier for the zipper to zip. Or, attach a zipper ring or large paper clip onto the tab, making it easier for your child to hold.

Zip my zipper? Children love the sound of the letter /z/, perhaps because it is the strongest sounding letter of the alphabet. Exaggerate the sound when your child is unzipping: "Unzip your zipper, Miss Zippity Zingzing. Zipping is zappy, zipping is fun!" Children enjoy saying funny-sounding words, just for the pleasure of acting silly.

Stimulation Techniques

From birth onward, your child's language skills have progressed in a rather orderly, standard sequence. This sequence is

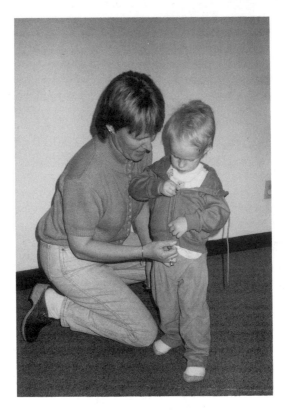

Zipping is challenging and fun.

fairly predictable, although each child may pass through each stage at a different rate. One child may be talking in three- and four-word sentences at 24 months, while another maybe at the two-word stage. Although individual differences are great, the pattern or sequence that children progress through is relatively stable.

Children appear to acquire a "rule" system that governs the way they combine words to make sentences. Once your child begins putting together phrases and sentences, she is following these basic rules of grammar, although it will take her some time to get all the rules right and put the words in the correct order.

While children are learning language, they will make many mistakes in putting sentences together, many of which are special and quite comical to adults. For example, when Amanda proudly showed mother her clean room, she said, "I picked up my toys all," instead of "I picked up all my toys."

Children learn that when talking about more than one object, the plural is formed by adding an /s/ or /z/ sound to the end of a word (of course they don't do this consciously). As a result, the child applies this rule to all objects, so that sheep becomes sheeps and mouse becomes mouses! The same is true for learning the rule of past tense, for which we add an /ed/ to the end of a word. In this case, children may say "goed" instead of "went," or "runned" instead of "ran." This just goes to show that your child is not simply copying what you say (you don't say mouses or goed!), but is also listening to her own ideas of how something should be said, based on the rule that's been incorporated in her mind. Pronouns are also confusing, probably because the meaning constantly changes depending on who is speaking (you or I?). Then there are constant pronouns like "he" and "she," and "him" and "her." "Him goed outside" and "her feeded the dogs" are typical patterns that are not really errors, but part of the learning process.

These differences in the 2½-year-old's language are all part of the normal progression through the complex task of language learning. Just as the adult practices his golf swing, your child practices talking, applying grammatical rules to her utterances and learning how to pronunciate words correctly. Her special speech at this stage is often amusing, and with patience and by setting a good example in your own speech, she will eventually learn the proper order and linguistic forms of the language in a natural way.

CHAPTER TWELVE

Creating Conversations
31–33 Months

Almost three! You and your child have come a long way together in such a short time. It is amazing the amount of language growth a child experiences before his third birthday. In another year, his understanding and use of language will closer approximate that of adults, and he will be fine-tuning these skills in the early elementary years.

In your conversations together, try to use more open ended statements and questions that will encourage your child to use more than one word in his responses. Now, you are encouraging more expansion and less simplicity in his talking. For example, if you ask, "Did you have fun at Grandma's?" you will get a "yes" response. However, if you ask, "What did you and Grandma do today?" your child's response will involve more words, as you are encouraging him to think and recall the events of his day. You can encourage more fruitful conversations, and encourage him to put his thoughts into words by the way you phrase your questions and comments. It may be helpful to begin your statements with:

- Tell me more . . .
- Try it and see . . .
- Let's find out . . .

- How did that feel . . . ?
- What do you think . . . ?
- How did that happen . . . ?
- What would you do if . . . ?

Another way to encourage creative conversation with children is to refrain from asking any questions at all! Simply talk with your child about one of your experiences ("Today I made such a silly mistake at the office . . . "), without confronting him or expecting a response. He may then feel free to ask you questions for you to elaborate on your story, or begin describing an event that he experienced during the day.

The typical three-year-old desires information, expansion, and elaboration on objects and events. He is eager to ask questions and seems to have a thirst for knowledge, wanting to know the names of things, the way they work, and why they work that way!

A child's sense of wonder can, at times, be exhausting: "What do bees eat?" "Where do rabbits sleep?" "Why did my bird die?" As you are assaulted with questions, questions, questions, try to be patient! Answering your child's questions transmits much useful information in new subject areas for him. Your answers don't have to be lengthy and philosophical; just simple and down-to-earth.

Note: If attempts to engage your child in conversation are met with silence, that's fine. Some children are quiet by nature, and their choice not to participate in the conversation should be respected.

Developmental Milestones

Understanding and Talking

- Understands questions that begin with "who," "what," "where," "whose," and "why"
- Understands the functions of objects ("What is a stove used for?" "What do we do with books?")

- Knows full name
- Comprehension of concepts expands: understands words like "around," "behind," "in front of," "in back of," and so forth
- Understands more descriptive words, such as "quiet," "loud," "fast," "slow," "careful," and so forth
- Understands the names of five or more familiar places, such as Grandma's, the store, Kelsey's house, outside
- Understands time-related words, such as "now," "later," "pretty soon," "tomorrow"
- Understands and responds appropriately to "my turn" and "your turn"
- Wants detailed explanations for things he sees
- Uses past tense with several verbs ("Justin jumped down") and applies the rule faithfully ("Hat falled off")
- Uses the articles "a" and "the" in sentences
- Makes a choice when you ask him a question, such as, "Do you want Cheerios or corn flakes?"
- Uses words that denote quantity, such as "some," "all," "one," "lots"
- Consistently speaks in three-word-plus sentences
- Uses other negatives in addition to "no," such as "don't," "can't," and "not"
- Makes sentences using the verb "is," as in, "Daddy is sleeping," or "That's mine"

Motor Skills

- Learns to pedal a small tricycle
- Can walk on a line, one foot in front of the other
- Alternates feet going up the stairs
- Still enjoys climbing and testing out motor abilities
- Can copy a circle and cross on paper

Toy Play

- Talks about events in dramatic play: "Here's the pie mommy made" (hands a flattened piece of playdough to his doll)

- Assigns roles to different characters ("I'm the daddy")
- Uses more props in play (stuffed animals, boxes, dolls, vehicles, dress-up clothes and costumes, child-sized household items like brooms, snow shovels, carpentry tools)
- Can put together three- and four-piece puzzles
- Stacks graduated rings according to size
- Plays with shape sorters (circles go in one hole, squares go in another hole, etc.)
- Enjoys lacing-cards, simple lotto matching games, small tricycles, tub toys with removable figures, small boats and cars, and short, simple, story books with repetition and familiar subjects

Playtime Activities

Obstacle Course

Using readily available objects around the house or day care, construct an obstacle course for your toddler. Explain to him that he must first listen to your direction, then do what he is asked to do.

Set up the following items on the floor to match these directions: "Stand on the paper, step over the pillow, crawl under the blanket, and sit inside the box." Walk your child through each direction, one at a time, until he understands what he is supposed to do. Then, make a game of it, giving him the challenge of carrying out the directions as quickly as he can.

After a few trials, let him complete the course without any verbal directions from you and see if he remembers what he did the first few times. Switch roles and see if he can give you one of the directions to carry out. He will verbalize one direction at a time: "Mommy, stand on the paper." Follow his direction, then go on to the next item. Encourage his verbalizations by saying, "OK, Justin, what do I do next? This is fun. What comes next?"

Make your directions more complicated according to the child's abilities. Most children nearing age three are able to remember three directions at a time without a repetition.

Animal Walk

Take turns acting out the various movements of different animals. Demonstrate first and ask your child to guess what animal you are.

Move your arms in a swimming motion and say, "I'm swimming, I'm swimming. What animal am I?" For a bird, flap your arms and walk on your tiptoes, making bird sounds. For a bear, take wide steps on all fours, making growling sounds. For an elephant, fold your hands together, extend your arms out, and sway them back and forth like an elephant's trunk. As you slow-

"I'm a dog!"

ly walk, give your child additional clues as to what animal you might be: "I love to eat peanuts. You have seen me at the zoo."

Take turns with your child and ask him to pretend he is an animal for you to guess. You may need to help him along at first by making simple suggestions: "Pretend you're a kitty cat," or "Pretend you're a dog." Follow up on this activity by planning a trip to the zoo or farm and talking about how animals move, what they eat, and how they live.

Brand New Words

Don't be afraid to introduce new, more descriptive words to your child, adding color to his vocabulary.

During mealtime, as you place a plate of food before him, describe it in many ways, using words he may not yet be familiar with.

- Macaroni and cheese is: delicious, smooth, creamy, steamy
- Jello is: light, soft, cool, red, wiggly
- Potato chips are: crunchy, brittle, salty, tasty

Don't shy away from lengthy words because your child does not yet understand them. "Interesting," "gigantic," "curious," "terrific"—kids love big, descriptive words. They are delighted to learn that the leafy, hanging plant in the kitchen is called a "rhododendron," and "galoshes" are really a pair of rubber boots! Continually talking to a child at his level only may contribute to creating a sterile, unimaginative vocabulary. Many children will rise up to the occasion as long as the big words are presented in a meaningful context. If your child likes dinosaurs, naming different types while looking at pictures is a good start (if you can pronounce them!).

Pantomime Time

As children play and replay common events in their world, they not only understand them better, but elaborate on the themes and gradually become more and more sophisticated in their play.

Two-years-olds understand the word "pretend" when it is used by an adult during play. The child gradually understands the difference between reality and fantasy; for example, he knows he's not really eating broccoli when you pretend to eat it from a magazine ad. In this type of play, no props are used. We simply pretend to carry out everyday experiences through pantomime.

Tell your child you are going to pretend together: "Let's pretend to take a bath, Justin. Scrubby, dubby, I'm taking a bath" (as mom exhuberantly pretends to wash her body).

Pretending to play horns.

CHAPTER TWELVE

You can take turns in this game, clapping for each other after each performance. Your child's turn will most likely be brief; clap for him, then announce it is your turn and he can be the audience. After a few turns, you can see if your child understands the big picture, namely, he knows when to watch, when to clap, and when to take his turn. Children catch on very quickly to this sequence of events.

Act out many daily experiences. This can become quite fun and silly; the sillier the better. Examples include going to bed, driving a car, eating supper, licking an ice cream cone, playing a horn, beating a drum, brushing your teeth, combing your hair, dumping sand out of your shoes, and blowing out candles on a birthday cake.

Scarf Dance

In your box of props for pretend play, include an assortment of scarves in many colors. Children find many different ways to use scarves in their imaginative play.

Direct a scarf dance for your child (or children; this is fun to do in a group). Hand him a scarf and experiment with its properties. Throw it up in the air and watch it fall. Describe your actions: "The scarf falls down slowly. Scarves are light and soft."

With a scarf or two in each hand, move your arms in many directions, creating patterns in the air. Swoop, twist, bend, and turn, and run with the scarves, with several in each hand. Pretend to be dancing, and impart to the children the feeling of lightness and floating with your whole body, describing as you go: "This feels light and soft. Let's dance light and soft."

Then change your expressions to dance hard and loud. Shake the scarves boldly, stomping your feet and striking out in different directions: "Now we're dancing hard and loud."

More than your words, the way in which you use your voice and body will give meaning to your actions. Use a light, breathy voice and slow, lofty movements when dancing softly,

Watch me whirl scarves.

and use a louder, punctuated voice and heavy, solid steps when dancing hard. Theatrics go a long way in enabling children to comprehend and use language effectively.

Creative rhythm activities also provide an emotional release for children. They are free to move and express themselves in a permissive atmosphere, experimenting with how their bodies move in space. Dancing also allows children the opportunity to develop poise and balance.

Storm Watchers

This activity is a little different in that, rather than directing and actually doing something, you are teaching your child to observe.

Storms are a wonderfully dramatic weather form that can

teach us a lot about our world, and ultimately ourselves. Weather affects our changes in mood and emotions, just as it changes other elements in nature.

Aware caregivers will draw a child's attention to storms. During the next thundershower, turn the lights out, open a window, and greet the storm with a sense of wonder. Sit near the window, or go out on an enclosed porch, and close your eyes. Talk to your child about what he hears. Distinguish thunder, trees blowing, and rain pattering on the roof.

Next, call your child's attention to how the storm smells. Take very deep breaths, filling your lungs with the smell of rain. Then, watch the storm, and talk about how it makes the trees and grass grow, how it forms puddles in the street, how the drops hit the sidewalk and the tops of cars.

If possible, dress your child appropriately and go out with an umbrella (when there's no lightning) and have fun in the rain. Dance and sing, spread your arms, feel the rain, and catch raindrops in your mouth.

Think about how this scenario compares with the scene in which an adult shuts the window, closes out the surroundings, and talks in disgust about the bad weather. Storms give us energy inside, and are a pleasurable learning experience for children.

Walk the Plank

Now that walking, running, and jumping are well established, give your child another small challenge to build upon his coordination and balance skills. As his coordination and balance mature, he will inevitably try more difficult movements and will learn to trust his body and senses.

See if he can balance and walk forward on a straight line. Walk along painted lines in parking lots, tape long lines on the sidewalk, or walk along a two-by-four board. As you "walk the plank," talk to him about balance. First, demonstrate it for him, extending your arms and exaggerating your movements as if

Keep your balance!

walking on a tightrope: "Walk on the line, Justin. See, you can balance. It takes work to balance, but you did it!" The concept of balance will be easy for him to learn as he experiences it with his whole body.

Sail the Balloon

Another full body movement activity that challenges your child to maintain his equilibrium is "Sail the Balloon." Keeping the balloon afloat will challenge his motor skills, as he holds his balance and reaches up with both hands.

Explain to him the object of the game: toss the balloon up in the air and try to keep it from touching the ground. Bat the balloon back and forth a few times first, describing how it floats effortlessly. Let it fall to the ground and say, "Uh oh, it hit the

Keeping the balloon afloat.

floor. Let's try and keep it *up*, Justin." Show him how to bat the balloon up and explain what you are doing: "Don't let the balloon hit the floor; hit the balloon *up*." Hit it over to him and let him try to bat at it while keeping his balance.

Each time the balloon hits the floor, describe the action: "Uh oh, it fell down, on the floor. Now what?" and wait for him to direct you in the game.

String Ring

You need only a ball of yarn and a little boy who wants to play at following your directions. Children easily learn to follow directions in their home or day care environment. "Take off your shoes," "Give the cup to Daddy," "Go get your coat," "Put my keys on the table" are all directions that a child learns by living in the context of everyday routines.

In this game, your child is challenged to follow directions that are not in his familiar context; rather, they are contrived out of context and constitute the playing of a game.

Make a circle on the floor with yarn or string. Stand inside the circle, and jump out. Ask your child to jump into the circle. Then, tell him to listen very carefully and see if he can do exactly what you say: "Do what I say, Justin. Ready?"

The directions test your child's ability to listen and respond to prepositional phrases: "Put one foot *in* the circle," "Put your hand *in* the circle," "Take your foot *out* of the circle," "Put both feet *in* the circle," and so on.

To further challenge his thinking skills, use a few of his familiar toys, asking him to put them in and take them out of the circle with your direction. Make a game out of it, challenging him to remember two items in a row: "Put the ball and the block *in* the circle. Good! Now take the ball and block *out* of the circle." Keep it very simple and lively, rather than mechanical, so as not to lose his interest.

Experiment with the string. Make a triangle on the floor; then change the shape and make a square. If you are really brave, give the entire ball of string to your youngster and let him create a collage in the house by stringing it along the floor and across the furniture. See what he can create without worrying about making a mess; remember, he can help clean things up, too!

What's It For?

All of the routine activities in a child's day, from dressing to eating, brushing teeth, playing, and socializing with others, gives him plenty of experience with understanding the use of objects. He now can name many objects, people, and events in

Point to the ones we wear.

his environment. To provide a thoughtful challenge, play a game that stimulates his ability to recognize an object by its function, rather than simply by its name.

Select a familiar book that has pictures of many different things: toys, foods, clothing, outdoor items, common objects, etc. Or use a catalog and look at the pictures together. Ask your child to point to the picture you name by its function (don't label it). For example, "Justin, what do we wear on our feet? Right! Shoes. Show me which one we cut with? Yes, a pair of scissors."

Collect four or five household objects, placing them on the table before your child, and play the same game. Ask him to pick the one used for "_____," and let him keep each object until the game is finished.

Other examples include: "Which one do we use to fix our hair?" "What do we ride on?" "What do we use to brush our teeth?" "Which one is used to sweep the floor?" "Which one do we use to drink our milk?" Your child understands verbs and makes an association between the use of the object and its name.

Finally, turn the game around and ask silly yes/no questions to further stimulate his thinking: "Do we wear a cake?" "Do we eat shoes?" "Do we fly in a car?" Repeat the question if your child doesn't understand, emphasizing the verb and giving him a puzzled look. These kinds of questions are sure to elicit plenty of giggles.

Activities in Your Daily Routines of Dressing, Feeding, and Bathing Your Child

All by Myself

By now, your child is able to dress independently—well, almost! He can slip his pants on, put on his socks, but still needs help getting the shirt over his head, fastening buttons, snapping snaps, and starting zippers.

Allow him to do as much of his dressing as he can on his own and make a game out of it: "Here are your clothes; can you dress all by yourself?" He won't do it all at first, but be sure to praise each and every gesture he makes at trying: "Wow, you're putting your pants on, all by yourself. Now what do we need? Yes, we need socks. Here are your blue socks. Can you put them on? Now what else do we need?"

You won't be dressing him quickly, as it will take time to observe and assist as needed, giving verbal encouragement on his successes. But, the extra time you occasionally take will pay off in the long run, as your child gains confidence in the process of learning self-care routines.

Set the Table

The 33-month-old can be a big help at mealtime. At the table, set up a model place setting for yourself and give your

Getting ready for dinner.

child what he needs to set a complete place setting (glass, plate, silverware, and napkin). Ask him to duplicate your setting. On occasion, purposely omit a fork or spoon and see if he will notice and ask you for another. Can he make all the settings match like the original?

Young children enjoy demonstrating their growing independence by helping with simple tasks. Helping set and clear the table may very well become one of his daily chores.

People Play

Pretending with small toy people in the bathtub is a fun way to encourage imaginative play and create dialogue between the characters. Fisher-Price makes very sturdy, colorful, toy people in various sizes for big and little hands to grasp.

Place the toy people on the sides of the tub and create dialogue for them as you move them about: "Here I go. I'm diving underwater. Kerplunk! I did a belly flop! Hurry, hurry, swim to the side." You won't have to confront or question your child at all to gain his participation. Most kids will join in the fun, and pretend the people are jumping, splashing, diving, and swimming from one end of the tub to the other.

Toy people, like puppets, are very useful in creating conversations because the toy places some distance between the child and the role of the toy. The child then feels less inhibited in acting out events.

Brush My Teeth

It is important to establish good oral hygiene habits in young children, starting from the time first teeth appear. Gauze is used to clean teeth when they first appear, and by age two most children enjoy experimenting with a soft toothbrush. By age three, your child may be more willing and capable of brushing his teeth all by himself.

Let him do the brushing without your interference, then briefly finish the job (it will take some time before he has the dexterity to brush the teeth well). Describe the sequence of events: "Now we need water for rinsing. Where's your cup? Turn on the water. Swish the water around in your mouth. Now spit it out."

Briefly talk about the importance of brushing teeth, and his eventual visit to the dentist for a check-up. You can play "dentist" together to familiarize him with the experience beforehand.

Stimulation Techniques

To further illustrate ways in which to maintain conversations with young children, consider the following two exam-

Are they sparkling and white?

ples. The first example illustrates an attentive caregiver who shows respect for the child's skill level and communicative skills. The second interaction is less fruitful and stifles further communication between caregiver and child.

Sarah is seated on the floor next to her Dad, contentedly playing with her favorite doll. Dad is simply observing, and from time to time he looks at Sarah, smiles, and comments about her play.

DAD: "You sure love your doll, Sarah. Is she tired and ready for bed?"

SARAH: "Uh huh. Night-night time for baby."

DAD (commenting on what Sarah is doing): "You're taking her shoes and socks off."

SARAH: "Yep. Baby's dress too; I can't do it!" (pulls at dress sleeve in frustration).

DAD: "Would you like some help?"

SARAH: "Uh huh. Take baby's dress off."

DAD (as he assists with dress): "Pull her arm out. Good. Now let's pull her other arm out. There, we did it."

SARAH: "We did it. Now you kiss her, Daddy" (hands doll to Dad).

DAD: (Smiles and kisses doll, and waits for Sarah's next response.)

In this conversation, Dad showed warmth and understanding as to his daughter's needs. He didn't dominate the conversation by telling her what to do and how to do it. He simply followed her lead, and commented in a helpful way about her initiations.

The next conversation, in contrast to the one above, is void of warmth. The parent takes complete control of the situation, thus stifling any further conversation. Justin is playing with a puzzle while his mother observes.

MOTHER: "Justin, that's the wrong piece. It won't fit in that space."

JUSTIN: (Ignores Mother and tries to make another piece fit.)

MOTHER: "Justin, come here and I'll show you."

JUSTIN: "No! I want do it!"

MOTHER: (Walks over to Justin and puts the right puzzle piece in for him.) "This one goes in this space. Now you try it."

JUSTIN: "No. I don't want it!" (gets up and stomps away).

This conversation lacks shared interaction, laughter, and warmth between the mother and child. The mother was not following the child's lead, or showing enough patience to follow his signals. She took control of the play situation, was not sensitive to Justin's feelings, and used no descriptive words (like naming the picture on the puzzle).

On the other hand, Sarah's Dad listened and watched his child for clues to her feelings. He made eye contact and smiled, showing acceptance of her play, and did not continually direct her next move. He also used descriptive language (talked about taking the baby's shoes off and pulling her arms out). Sarah's Dad described what Sarah was doing ("You're taking her shoes off") and commented on her feelings ("You sure love your baby") as well.

Using descriptive language, commenting on what your child is doing, and asking beforehand if he'd like assistance with a toy builds mutual respect and positive feelings between the parent and child. Too much commanding always diminishes communication, and puts the child in a defensive position.

Keep the doors of communication open, starting now. As a result, your job as a parent in the years to come will reap greater successes, and your relationship with your child will be far more fruitful and satisfying.

CHAPTER THIRTEEN

Problem Solving
34–36 Months

Three years old already? It's hard to believe your little wonder has grown up so fast and has accomplished so much. Your child now understands most of what adults say, and her use of new words is expanding readily. She knows how to use language to get what she wants, to comment on what she sees, and to fantasize familiar experiences in her play. She is beginning to express her thoughts and feelings more accurately, and is also accumulating literacy readiness skills that will be a stepping stone for later reading and writing in the elementary school years.

Encouraging the three-year-old to solve problems is a good way to build upon and exercise her language skills in the preschool years. Now that your child frequently asks, "Why?" or "What's that?" it may be tempting for you to supply a quick answer. Why not try encouraging her to think of possible solutions or outcomes in different situations?

When you come across a problem during the day, state what the problem is, and together think of different ways to solve it. For example, you observe that two children want to play with the same toy. Instead of taking control and solving the problem for them, ask your three-year-old to think of ways, other than fighting, that the problem could be solved. At first, you will need to be a good model and make suggestions for her: "Maybe we could cooperate and play together, or maybe we could set a timer and take turns with the toy. What do you think?" Asking children to help come up with a solution takes some of the pressure off of you to always be in control, and places some responsibility on them to think for themselves. Children learn from their mistakes and experiences, continually building on what they already know. It is wise to give your child the opportunity to apply these facts and principles in her daily life.

This process will take time to accomplish, but starting at the three-year-age level is not too early to begin. Once your child has internalized the fact that she carries some of the responsibility to work things out, she will begin making suggestions on her own and set a good example for other children in social situations. Sometimes, of course, there isn't time to find answers together, and succinct explanations will do in satisfying her immediate needs.

Developmental Milestones

Understanding and Talking

- Knows full name, sex, and age
- Listens and can be reasoned with
- Follows commands involving two unrelated actions such as, "Flush the toilet, and then go find your hairbrush"
- Can differentiate between words that are singular or plural, as in "Get the plate" and "Get the plates"
- Understands a greater number of descriptive words, such as "noisy," "delicious," "small," "wet," and so forth.
- Sentences may be six words in length or more
- Speaking vocabulary may be close to 1000 words
- Can count to three

- Uses past and future verb tenses
- Speaking vocabulary becomes more descriptive: can talk about shapes, sizes, textures, and colors (although not always accurately)
- May use "and" to connect compound sentences
- Uses polite forms such a "please" and "thank you"
- Relates immediate experiences to family members
- Answers yes/no questions with accuracy
- Converses in complete sentences that are 80 percent understandable to the listener
- "Plays" with words and creates humorous statements, such as, "My sock goes on my nose!"
- Uses the words "here" and "there" to describe a location
- Tries to control situations using words, as in, "You can't have that," "I don't want to," "Put it down!"

Motor Skills

- Runs smoothly and easily
- Learns to catch smaller balls (tennis, softballs)
- Broad-jumps, or bunny-hops with both feet together
- Can jump over an object on the ground
- Enjoys outdoor equipment, such as jungle gyms, ladders, and swingsets
- Alternates feet walking downstairs
- Builds a tower with 10 or more blocks
- Scribbling becomes more controlled, with better defined strokes

Toy Play

- Enjoys familiar, realistic-looking scenes (farm, garage, airport) with multiple pieces and moving parts

- Uses blocks in imaginative play (builds enclosures for vehicles and dolls)
- Uses puppets and dolls as partners in play and assigns them specific roles (pretends that puppets or dolls are conversing with each other)
- Puzzles, shape balls, books, picture cards, crayons, and assorted art materials are of interest
- Enjoys a variety of props (household items used for dress-up, housecleaning, transportation, telephoning, eating, shopping, going to the doctor, etc.) in extended make-believe play
- Enjoys color/picture dominoes and lotto games
- Enjoys ride-on toys propelled by bouncing up and down, climbing structures and slides, and swings with curved, soft seats
- Likes lacing-cards or a wooden shoe for lacing
- Enjoys musical instruments in addition to horns and whistles
- Likes simple story books, pop-up books, and hidden picture books

Playtime Activities

Tape Recorder Fun

To get a permanent record of your child's language skills over time, make an audio tape of her talking. (Be sure to label your tape, for example, "Sarah, 3 years old, August 1990.) Her language skills will never progress any faster than in these first three years of life, and this tape will become an irreplaceable treasure for both of you.

Children are fascinated by the sound of their own voices. Many children (and adults) "clam up" when asked to speak directly into a tape recorder, so make your taping session as inconspicuous as possible. Set up puppet play, or sit down together and look at a book, talking about the pictures while you are recording.

"Hello. My name is Mark."

Some children enjoy hamming it up, and don't mind being directly confronted and questioned while their voices are being taped. Use your own judgment on how to encourage your child's participation. Once she hears her voice played back, she'll be hooked!

Outdoor Discoveries

Each time you go for a walk with your child, turn it into an activity of discovery. Earlier, on your outdoor adventures, you gave objects and experiences labels, so that your child would learn the names of things. Now, her thinking is becoming more abstract, and you may expand your descriptions, talk about the relationships between objects, and encourage her to categorize them in her mind.

The water feels cold.

Go for a walk together. If you live in the city, ask your child to show you all the things she sees with wheels. Play the "I see . . ." game and get her started by saying, "Let's look for things with wheels. I see a car. A car has wheels. What else do you see that has wheels? Yes, a garbage truck. Look, I see a bicycle . . ."

Each time, pursue another category. Find animals, different flowers, road signs, different types of bugs, things that are tall, things that make noise, things that fly, and things that go fast. This is even fun for adults as it forces one to look at things from a slightly different perspective.

Now your child can make differentiations between objects. She used to overextend a word, thinking that, for example, all round things were called balls, or every four-legged animal was called a doggie. Now she understands that those same round objects (the moon and a ball, for example) have many other properties and uses that make them different objects, bearing distinctive names. This is quite a leap in thinking from those days of early learning.

A Special Book

Children can be exposed to literacy at a very early age, even though they are yet unable to read and write. Initially, children randomly scribble for pleasure, without intention of meaning anything. As they become exposed to written symbols, they continue to scribble, but pretend the scribble has meaning and that adults can read it! Later still, the four-year-old begins to write mock messages and experiments (albeit imprecisely) with letter forms.

Using a spiral notebook, explain to your child that this special book will be made up of letters that the both of you have written back and forth to each other. Start out with a very simple, one-sentence letter to your child: "Dear Sarah, I love you." Point to the words as you read the letter to her. Then encourage her to write a letter to you on the following page. She will make marks on the page and draw lines and circles. Pretend to read her letter, and thank her for her efforts. If desired, you could even make a pretend mailbox out of an old shoebox, and ask her to periodically check and see if there is any mail for her.

Another special book activity requires the parent to write down the child's exact words on a piece of paper, and then read the words back to the child. Talk with the child about a recent experience, and write down what she says ("I goed to the zoo. I seed two polar bears"). If she uses the incorrect form of a word, write it down the correct way in her sentence and read it aloud, without calling attention to it. This way you are giving her the correct example, and she will gradually come to use the proper forms on her own.

Most kids are enthralled with stories comprised of their own words. Once you have accumulated a few pages of the child's experiences, staple them together and label it, "Sarah's Book."

Keep a variety of writing materials on hand for your three-year-old. Crayons, pencils, index cards, envelopes, ruled paper, scrap paper, and colorful stickers are simple items that will stimulate her language growth as she experiments with them, pretending to write letters, draw, and play school.

Parts of a Whole

As your child grows, she begins to notice more and more details in the things she sees and understands. Labeling and mentally organizing objects and experiences helps her to develop memory skills, and she comes to understand how the many different parts of an object or experience make up the whole.

Where is the horse's tail?

You can exercise this skill by calling attention to the parts of a whole by looking at picture books and asking for details: "Look, Sarah, can you find the wheels on the bus? Where's the nose on the doggie? Where's the tail of the horse? Find the door on the car. Where's a window on the house? Point to the baby's ear."

Three-year-olds are ready for more expansion and elaboration about things in their world. Follow your child's cues, being careful not to bombard her with information that does not interest her. When you do find something that especially peaks her interest, give her expanded information on the subject, in a simple and natural way.

Puzzle Play

Working puzzles provides additional exercise in understanding how many parts make up a whole. Developing eye–hand coordination and expanding vocabulary are also valuable by-products of puzzle play.

Choose puzzles with three or four pieces representing common objects, toys, or animals. The two-year-old can work a puzzle in which each piece represents an entire object (a puzzle with an apple and a banana, for example). At three, however, your child is ready to assemble three or four related pieces that make a whole picture. Keep your puzzle selections simple, perhaps choosing a picture of a dog, with the pieces being the head, tail, body, and legs.

Name the picture of the puzzle and the pieces: "Let's play with the giraffe puzzle. Where's the giraffe's long neck? I wonder where that piece goes." Let your child experiment on her own. Figuring out puzzles requires much trial and error, and your child will be very pleased with herself when she succeeds.

If assistance is needed, watch what your child is doing and keep your directions to a minimum. You could guide her hand close to the correct spot and wait for her to see the connection.

I can work a puzzle.

Or ask her to turn the piece around a little bit so that it fits properly. Give her plenty of time to try and figure it out on her own, without undue frustration.

Sandpaper Circles

Sandpaper provides an excellent sensory medium for your child to explore. With crayons and sheets of sandpaper, draw a simple shape, like a circle. Ask your child to trace the circle with her finger: "I drew a circle. Let's make a circle with your finger. Slowly, round and round. My, that feels rough!"

On another piece of sandpaper, have your child draw a circle. Ask her to trace the circle with her finger again, as you describe the sensations: "It feels kind of bumpy!"

Turn the sandpaper over and have her feel the surface with

This paper feels rough.

her finger: "This side feels smooth. Can we draw on this side too? Let's give it a try."

Let her experiment on her own, using both sides of the paper and feeling the differences in texture with her finger and crayon.

Watering Plants

Doing simple chores around the home or day care provides a myriad of language learning opportunities for little ones. Let

Watering thirsty plants.

your child help you tend to your plants. During this activity, you can talk to her about how plants grow, blossom, and later die. Show her how little changes occur in their growth. Talk to her about stems, roots, and leaves.

Provide a spray bottle and show her how to spray the leaves. Most children love spraying, and you can talk about thirsty plants, and how they need water to grow big and tall. Give her a small cup filled with water and talk about dry vs. wet. Let her feel the dry dirt: "Uh oh. The soil is dry. This plant must be thirsty. Can you pour the water in for me?"

If your child would like to nurture her own plant, fill a styrofoam cup with dirt and let her sprinkle in grass seeds. After daily watering, she will see the process of growth unfold as the grass sprouts. Draw a face on the cup so that it resembles a person's head with hair (grass) growing on top! Preschoolers are delighted with this activity, and the opportunities for informal language learning are endless.

Brain Teasers

Provide an activity that will require your child to listen carefully, using familiar items in the home or day care. With a block and cup, see how well she can carry out your directions as you present them in a game-like manner.

Ask her to follow several directions and deliver these slowly, one at a time: "Sarah, put the block *in* the cup. Good! Now take it *out*, and let's play again. Put the block *under* the cup. Yes! OK. (Most kids put the block in first, then turn the cup over, rather than set the block on the table and place the cup over the top.) Sarah, can you put the block in *back* of the cup? Yes! Now put the block *in front* of the cup. OK, you're really listening well."

Exaggerate the prepositions or words that label the location in your sentence. If your child isn't familiar with them, show her where to place the block as you are naming the location.

In context, your child understands many locator words. She understands when you ask her to get her shoes from under her bed, or put the wastebasket under the sink. Isolating the preposition and asking a less familiar direction (though still using the block and cup) tests her ability to really understand the direction and focus on the smaller words in the sentence.

Make directions more difficult as you see fit, adding another cup and asking her to put the block between the cups, or asking her to give you one of the cups and put the other one in her lap. She will be ready for these types of lengthier directions in the months ahead. Other locator words that she may be familiar with now include "up" and "over," "inside," and "next to."

Rhyme Time

A parent is most often aware of how her child uses language, how she puts words together to make sentences and produces speech sounds well enough to be understood by others. A good way to practice combining words into sentences is through rhyme games. Words are fun and most children adore silly sounds. Preschoolers especially enjoy making up nonsense rhymes as they experiment with language.

Give your child several examples to get the ball rolling. Use her name to begin with: "Sarah, kara, mara, dara. We can make up lots of silly words." Try "Mary, Berry, Sheri, Kari" or "Daddy, baddy, maddy, faddy." Nonsense words are delightful.

Sing simple rhyming songs while you are riding in the car, giving a bath, and fixing a meal. Songs like "Wheels on the Bus" and "Twinkle, Twinkle, Little Star" become favorites by virture of the repetition and sing-song quality that little ones love.

Predictable pattern books provide many examples of silly words and repetitive sentence patterns. Examples of books that utilize repetitive sentences include:

- *She'll be comin' round the mountain* by Robert Quackenbush.
- *Who, said Sue, said whoo?* by Ellen Raskin.
- *The three little pigs,* by Edda Reinl.
- *Old mother middle-muddle,* by Bill Martin, Jr.
- *One, two, buckle my shoe,* by William Stobbs.

Also be on the lookout for Dr. Seuss books, which continue to be a source of great entertainment for older children, as well as adults.

Even though your child may not understand all the words in the stories, she will enjoy the sounds and rhythms inherent in rhyming and predictable pattern books.

Outdoor Fun Run

Your runner is on the loose, and she is becoming increasingly more adept at running around and stepping over obstacles, turning corners, and stopping on a dime. Her motor coordination, balance, and ability to plan a route from point a to point z is steadily maturing.

Provide ample outdoor activities that will stimulate her motor skills and provide an interesting challenge. Pick a grassy spot and outline a path with a thin line of flour for her to follow. Make circles or zigzags. Hold her hand as you follow the line, weaving in and out wherever it leads you. Have her be the leader and follow at her pace.

Set up three or four boxes in a line and have her zigzag between them as fast as she can. Pretend to be a bunny rabbit and hop on two feet between them. Get dizzy together running in circles, falling down in the grass, and enjoying the moment.

See if she can follow your directions: "Run fast. Walk slowly. Hop on both feet. Follow me. Stop! Pretend you're a statue. Stand still." Describe and follow her movements, letting her be the leader from time to time in your play.

Activities in Your Daily Routines of Dressing, Feeding, and Bathing Your Child

Pick My Own Clothes

Challenge your child to get all items of clothing needed for the day on her own. By now, she probably knows where each item is kept. If she can reach her drawer, ask her to pick out a pair of pants and socks, then a shirt and underwear. Point out the colors she chooses: "Oh, your red shirt. That's a good choice." Don't worry about her unfolding other clothes; show her how to neatly fold things, but don't expect neatness! Praise her for picking her clothes out all by herself, and assist only when necessary in putting them on, even though she may be somewhat awkward at it.

Follow up your discussion on clothes by providing paper dolls with an assortment of paper clothes to wear. You can trace simple pictures of people from catalogs, cut them out, and mount them on plain paper. Then cut out clothing items from the same catalog and let your child dress the doll as she pleases.

Dad helps choosing clothes.

(Book and grocery stores often sell prepackaged paper doll cut-outs.) Talk about the colors of the clothing and the types of clothes worn in different seasons.

Cut, Slice, and Peel

Young children enjoy trying to cut with a knife or scissors, and this is perfectly fine for the three-year-old, *as long as she is supervised.* Rather than instill fear by insisting a child will cut herself, take the time to explain the uses of these tools, emphasizing that they can only be used with an adult present.

Let your child slice a banana. Since bananas are soft, this will be easy and she will learn how to handle the knife properly: "Let's slice the banana, Sarah. Watch me first and then you can try. That's very good. Let's count our slices: one, two, three, four!"

Let her practice from time to time while you are preparing

meals. Start with soft foods first, then later let her help you chop vegetables or try peeling potatoes. (This will be awkward for her, but very challenging and fun!) While you are working together, talk about the taste and smell of the foods, and how you best like them prepared. Talk about their colors and textures, and ask her what are her favorite foods. Since eating is a favorite play theme for children, you will have no difficulty involving your child in its preparation (all it takes is patience and some extra time).

Peanut Butter and Jelly Sandwiches

Invite your child to make her own lunch! Pose the question, "What do we need to make peanut butter and jelly sandwiches?" See if she can name all the necessary items: a plate, two slices of bread, a knife, and the jars of peanut butter and jelly.

My favorite lunch: P. B. & J's!

Let her hold the bread and spread the peanut butter and jelly. She will delight in this accomplishment. Spreading with the knife will be awkward at first because her manual dexterity is not fully developed, but her feelings of self-worth and achievement in making her own lunch is worth the small mess she may create. Give her the opportunity to experience independence such as this, in small doses, and she will happily fulfill your expectations.

I'm a Fish

During bathtub play, have your child lie flat on her tummy, with your hand supporting her chest if necessary. Encourage her to pretend to be a fish: "You're a fish, Sarah. Swim like a fish. Kick your feet!" Show her how to use her arms for swimming. Share your own stories of learning how to swim.

Expect to get thoroughly splashed during all the excitement. It may be some time before your child will be able to coordinate these movements into smooth, efficient swimming. In the meantime, you can talk about and practice vigorous arm and leg movements, blow bubbles on the surface of the water, and just have plain fun. (Many pools offer swimming classes for toddlers whose parents are interested in a structured teaching approach.)

Swimming offers excellent opportunities for total body exercise and water play. Young children love playing and splashing in the water, sharing this special quality time with one or both parents. If using a pool, make it a pleasurable experience, without pushing or forcing her to swim or make "correct" movements. Easing her into the water, reassuring her, and acknowledging any fears will help her gain confidence in the water.

Animal Placemats

Colorful, vinyl placemats are a welcome sight to the three-year-old's table setting, providing yet another language learning experience and topic of conversation for the whole family.

Choose placemats with pictures of animals and, during mealtime, talk about the animal each person has under his plate: "The hippopotamus is so fat! Look at his big teeth. He's chewing on some grass. How big is a hippopotamus? Can you say that word?"

Let your child set out placemats and decide which member of the family will receive which animal: "Tonight, Daddy gets the dog. Mom gets the giraffe." Talk about which animal each of you likes best and why.

Collect placemats from restaurants (which often provide more than one upon request) and use them the next night after dining out. They will remind your child of where you dined and what you had for dinner, introducing many more topics of conversation and items of interest that she may remember from the night before. (Don't expect her to remember details from last week, however. Stick with the very recent past for now.)

Make your own placemats and label them with each family member's name. She will soon come to recognize the names and place the mats accordingly.

Stimulation Techniques

The three-year-old child is a joy and a challenge to live and learn with. She uses her ever-increasing language skills to tell stories, enrich her friendships with others, describe past experiences, and even share secrets! She can learn a great deal playing with other children her age, and is beginning to take notice of more people and places outside of her immediate home boundaries. This is clearly evident while driving in a car with a three-year-old. People, places, and unusual, as well as familiar, sights peak her interest.

You, the parent, or primary caregiver, have contributed a great deal to the unfolding of your child's language and personality. Simply supplying children with new toys and educational experiences, in the absence of your attention, falls short of the mark. Children want their parent's attention, to do simple things like reading books, cooking, singing, taking a walk, and playing together outdoors. Taking a small amount of your time every day to play with your child in a natural way contributes to functional communication development.

Keep in mind that exposing your three-year-old to different speaking styles is also worthwhile. In your personal life, you talk differently to your spouse than to a client in a business relationship. The style of speech you use with your three-year-old differs from that which is directed exclusively to your next door neighbor. Children can benefit from hearing the differences between using easygoing family style talk and the speaking styles, dialects, and even foreign languages overheard in the public arena.

One last suggestion that your three-year-old will love: each night, as you tuck her into bed, say, "Tell me three things that made you happy today." What will she say? She will name those very simple things that occurred as she interacted with a loving caregiver: "Molly kissed my boo-boo. She gave me a Bandaid. Me and Clara readed books!"

In these many small ways, we learn to celebrate our lives with our children each and every day. By sharing experiences with children, we expose them to language, which gives rise to all our thoughts. Through language, a child's ever-expanding awareness unfolds, and is one of the greatest joys an observant parent can behold.

CHAPTER FOURTEEN

Parents' Questions

My mother-in-law says I should not use baby talk with my 5-month-old son. Am I teaching him incorrect language usage when I use baby talk?

The answer to this question may depend on your style of parenting and perception of how children learn. If you do not view babies as "empty slates," and understand that whatever you write on the chalkboard will be imbued with them for life, you will naturally be careful about what you say and how you say it.

In the past, baby talk was highly discouraged by experts, but recent theories about how babies learn point to the advantages. At present, it is widely known that babies initially learn the elements of language through intonational patterns imposed upon the adult's speech. For example, you look at your baby, smile, and say in a sing-song way, "Hi Sweetie, cutie widdle baby." Baby is not tuning into the fact that you said "widdle" for "little"; rather, he comes to understand that what you have said is a term of endearment. For some parents, using baby talk is their way of conveying closeness and warmth, and will not cause a baby to eventually speak incorrectly.

Speaking to a four-month-old baby in this way is natural. However, speaking to a three-year-old in baby talk is not natural. Often children will use baby talk long after they are capable of using correct speech. Perhaps the child is regressing in language skills because of an unusually stressful situation: a recent move, divorce, or entry into kindergarten. This is his way of telling you that growing up is difficult and it is more comfortable being a baby again. These regressions rarely last very long.

When an older child slips back into baby talk, the best you can do is simply rephrase his sentence and use correct English without passing judgment on his feelings.

My husband doesn't pay much attention to our 4-month-old son, although he's wonderful with our older son, who is two. Perhaps he feels that until the baby can talk, he need not talk to him?

Certainly your husband's attitude will not deter from your son's acquisition of speech and language skills. It may be that your husband feels uncomfortable conversing until the dialogue becomes a two-way street (and in a way it does, only not so much with words).

In our culture, babies are thought to need both mothers and fathers. However, in other cultures, men are often absent and working for months at a time, and this is considered normal. Perhaps your husband feels that at this time the mother is to take care of the baby's needs, and that his role to intervene in conversation and play will follow when the baby is a bit older.

What your husband does contribute by interacting with your son in infancy is affection and attention. Babies whose fathers talk and play with them, handle them, and show patience with their fussy behaviors develop intense and early attachments. These attachments then give the baby the confidence to more readily explore inanimate objects when he starts crawling and walking, which in turn makes a contribution to promoting his mental skills.

Discuss your feelings with your husband. It may not occur to him that the baby needs and loves his attention. Once he breaks through the wall of this misperception, he will be rewarded with the joys of getting to know his son early on.

Do children who talk more have higher IQs than other children?

No, not necessarily. Just because a child is late in speaking does not indicate depressed intellectual skills. Each child progresses at his own rate; some children speak in sentences very early, and others wait until around 2½ or 3 years of age.

In the elementary school years, children with high IQs tend to have richer vocabularies, use lengthier sentences, and possess even better pronunciation skills than children with lower IQs. But this may be attributable to the fact that IQ tests rely most heavily on a child's verbal ability. Thus, his scores will reflect his verbal skills, not his intellectual capacity. Many late talkers may have advanced skills in other areas, such as mathematics or creative problem solving.

Do firstborn children generally have more advanced language skills than those born later?

The research does not totally substantiate this claim, because there are so many uncontrolled variables. Perhaps a firstborn speaks better because he has spent more undivided time with adults before his siblings came along. If he comes from a small family, perhaps he has been exposed predominantly to adult language, and this has had an effect on his precocious language development.

Firstborns do not necessarily possess greater language skills. In fact, often the second born is more talkative because the inverse is true; he has learned a great deal from his older brothers and sisters.

My husband speaks English, and I speak both English and Spanish. Will it be too difficult for my baby to learn both languages simultaneously?

This decision is solely up to the parents, as the evidence is not clear-cut that bilingualism is problematic. Learning another language is certainly a highly valuable skill, and should not be discouraged in young children.

The studies do show, however, that children who learn two languages simultaneously will learn them both somewhat slower than a child learning only one language at a time. The implications of this suggest that it may be more beneficial to teach a child a second language after he is a few years old, when one language has already been well-established.

Often bilingual parents will speak to their children in both languages simultaneously, using English and Spanish, for example, in the same sentence, or even mixing syllables. The child may then appear to learn the individual languages at a slower rate than his monolingual counterpart, but in adulthood, both languages may be intact in his repertoire.

My firstborn child, a girl, spoke much sooner than my son who is very quiet and keeps to himself at 2½ years of age. Do girls just naturally acquire language at a faster rate than boys?

It has been a long-held belief that girls progress faster in language, although recent research does not support this conclusively. When looking at groups of children, one can make the observation that boys tend to be more physically active than girls, and girls more verbally precocious than boys. Upon individual inspection, however, one sees many children who do not fit this pattern. Some boys are gentle and quiet; some girls are feisty and active. Whether there are environmental influences or differences in brain chemistry that generate language learning differences in boys and girls has not yet been determined by researchers.

Since your little girl was the firstborn, she may have had an advantage because she did not have to compete with siblings to be included in conversations, and had more undivided attention from you and your husband. Your son's personality and style is also a factor. His temperament may simply dictate that he will be quiet and more self-oriented than his talkative sister.

What has been found to be true is that many more boys are diagnosed with speech and language disorders than girls. Special education programs enroll more boys than girls in their classes. Over half of the children diagnosed with speech problems are boys, and close to 90 percent of children who stutter are also boys. The reasons for this are not known. Some experts believe this may be due to the increased expectations our society places on boys to perform in all areas of life—language learning included.

CHAPTER FIFTEEN

Is My Baby Okay?

Spotting Potential Problems in Your Child's Speech and Language Development

Naturally, a parent is inclined to observe her child's behavior and wonder from time to time if the child is progressing normally in his development. A mother notes that her 8-month-old hasn't started crawling, yet a friend's baby of 9 months is already pulling up to a stand. A father notices other two-year-olds at day care talking in three-word phrases, yet his child is still in the single-word phase. These are normal feelings that all parents share as they discuss developmental milestones with other parents and make comparisons in their minds.

The most important precursor to language development in infancy is that of making eye contact and interacting with caregivers. Looking, touching, and talking with your baby should result in his gradually becoming a social partner in your games, reciprocating with smiles, vocalizations, and eventually words. Through these interactions, the onset of language has begun. Most children effortlessly mature through these stages just as they learn to crawl, walk, then run.

A small percentage of children, however, are eventually

diagnosed with speech and language problems. Recognizing these problems and planning a program of intervention are the first steps to overcoming them.

Language Delay

Naturally, if your child is not saying any words at 14 months of age, you will wonder about his development. Perhaps you have observed other children his age using many words to get their needs met, and you feel something may be wrong. There is so much variability among children's language learning that some children simply do not express themselves until later on, while others are verbally precocious.

Talk to other mothers about your dilemma and ask yourself questions. Even though your child does not use real words, does he communicate in other ways? Does he use consistent sound combinations for words, does he gesture and point, make sounds, or perhaps let an older sibling do all his talking for him? On the average, first words occur between 10 and 14 months (this is quite a range). Although average time frames are not absolute, they do have their place. Averages give us a range and means with which to spot potential difficulties before they turn into full-blown problems.

Wait a few months and, if you feel at that time that not much progress has been made, ask your pediatrician for a referral to a speech–language pathologist. She will be able to assist you in determining the range in which your child functions in terms of all aspects of his speech, language, and communication development, as well as possibly differentiate a disorder from a delay.

In most cases, a child is simply developing a little later than his counterparts, and in his own time will catch up. In a small percentage, however, an authentic language delay may be evidenced. A child with a language delay may not begin to use words clearly until three years of age or older. He may have difficulty comprehending the speech of others. His vocabulary, syntax, and articulation of speech may lag far behind children of similar age. Determining the cause of a language delay in an otherwise normally developing child is, more often than not, very unclear.

Sometimes delays are due to medical complications, such as prematurity at birth. Children with hearing problems also show evidence of language delay. In most cases, however, there are no obvious medical reasons for unsuccessful language learning and no single cause that can be attributed to the failure of language to progress normally. It is widely recognized, however, that the earlier a problem is discovered and treated, the better the child's prognosis for increased language learning. Most children enjoy a trouble-free period of language acquisition, but if you suspect there is a problem, obtain a speech and hearing test for your child. You should obtain a speech and hearing test for your child if:

1. He is not using any words by two years of age
2. His speech cannot be understood at three years of age (many consonant sounds are omitted, or he uses only vowels)
3. He is not using more than two- or three-word phrases at three years of age
4. His vocal quality is very hoarse, harsh, or nasal (sounds likes he is talking through his nose)
5. He has a history of recurrent ear infections, which could result in a language delay due to intermittent hearing acuity.

Hearing Problems

Children with hearing problems are initially at a disadvantage in developing language skills. In the critical early language learning years from birth to three years, a child without hearing has difficulty building receptive language, which is the basis of his understanding of the world. Serious speech difficulties are also a by-product of total or partial deafness.

Parents and teachers of hearing-impaired children can make extraordinary strides in teaching them to develop speech and language skills. However, timing is a critical factor. The sooner the diagnosis is made and a treatment plan administered, the better the child's chances for success.

You can crudely test your infant's hearing ability by making noises on either side of him (see "Sounds in the Kitchen" activity) and observing how he responds. How your child reacts to sound matures as he grows. Check your baby's behaviors at the following intervals.

3 months—Baby is startled by loud sounds, and slowly turns in the general direction of a sound
6 months—Looks in general direction of a sound with head and eyes more specifically; responds to mother's voice
9 months—Baby quickly looks directly to the sound source
12 months—If playing with a toy or concentrating on something, baby can now voluntarily ignore a sound; thus, a hearing loss may be harder to detect

If you suspect a hearing loss, ask your pediatrician for a referral to a hearing specialist (audiologist).

Disfluent Speech

True stuttering behaviors affect only about one percent of the population. What many parents label as stuttering may be referred to as normal disfluencies that nearly half of all preschoolers pass through as they acquire language skills.

From two to four years of age, many children pass through this stage of normal disfluent speech. A three-year-old who says, "mmmm . . . mama," repeating the first sound does not necessarily stutter. Also, the child who hesitates and pauses, "I want some . . . um . . . raisins," may not actually be stuttering.

These normal disfluencies are thought to occur because children in this critical stage of language development are trying to express ideas faster than they are able to form words. Perhaps the child wants to express an emotion, but cannot come up with the right words. Or, he has many things to tell you, and becomes overly excited in his attempts. Trying to use new vocabulary words, asking a question, or forming a complex sentence may all cause disfluent speech. Perhaps the child must constantly struggle to obtain attention from adults due to competition with siblings, becoming nervous and excitable when trying to gain the floor.

You can be of help to your child when disfluencies occur. Avoid overcorrecting his speech or telling him to start all over. If a 2½-year-old is constantly corrected, he will become self-conscious, and a vicious cycle begins: The parent corrects the child, and the child tries harder to produce fluent speech in his need for approval. As a result, he may become anxious (because the parent is anxious) and his speech breaks down even more.

To reduce the child's chances of developing stuttering behaviors, the following suggestions are worthwhile.

1. Slow down your rate of speech; most children will automatically match the speech rate of those around them.
2. Pay attention to *what* your child is saying, not *how* he is saying it. Give him time to finish what he has to say without rushing him.
3. Watch your nonverbal behaviors. Try not to show impatience or disapproval through body movements or facial expressions. Very young children can read and internalize how the adults around them feel. Children know when feelings and emotions are negative.
4. Don't demand that your child perform talking for others, for example, singing songs or reciting jingles. Constantly

telling a child to say "thank you" or "tell the pastor 'goodbye' " is also artificial.

5. Simplify your grammar and sentence length. Two- and three-year-olds need time to process information, and lengthy directions and high expectations to perform are stressful. Stress is manifest in broken speech patterns.

6. Above all, accept the way your child speaks and let him know he is succeeding whenever possible. So that he does not become uncomfortable about talking, refrain from discussing his disfluencies with another adult in his presence.

Unfortunately, sometimes a child's speech does turn into full-blown stuttering behaviors. Normal disfluencies and stuttering behaviors can be distinguished by their frequency and severity. If, after the age of three, your child still exhibits disfluencies that appear to increase over time, alerting your pediatrician and obtaining a speech evaluation is highly recommended.

Voice Problems

The two- to three-year-old child most likely imitates the voice he hears most, namely, mother's, father's, or the day-care provider's. Children can copy harsh, rough voices, or use excessive loudness if adults around them do so. Most common is misuse of the voice by yelling or shouting, which often occurs between little boys and their mothers.

Irritation of the vocal cords is caused by constant shouting, which can result in vocal nodules (small growths on the vocal cords). Usually these growths disappear if the yelling decreases. Sometimes, however, surgery is required when vocal misuse continues over many months.

If your child's voice undergoes a noticeable change, and the change lasts for several weeks, a visit to the otolaryngologist (ear, nose, and throat doctor) is suggested. Be aware of excessively harsh, hoarse, or nasal speech which may point to a voice problem.

Articulation of Speech Sounds

Parents easily recognize that errors in pronunciation or articulation are normal in young children. From cooing to babbling, from forming consistent sound combinations for words to the actual words themselves, children progress along a path of skills that lead to intelligible speech. But how long speech sound errors persist may be the puzzling question for many parents.

Articulating speech sounds requires coordination of the speech articulators (tongue, lips, teeth, and oral cavity) and breathing apparatus; all working in synchrony to form sounds into words. Speech sound development progresses in a somewhat orderly fashion, in which one can predict which sounds will develop first, and which ones will come later. Baby's babblings and early words include the easy sounds (ma, pa, ba) which require the lips and larynx (voice box) to produce. Other sounds require much more coordination of the tongue, lips, and teeth and are more difficult for a child to accurately produce.

At three years of age and older, most children pronounce all the vowel sounds and some of the consonants correctly, rendering their speech about 80 percent intelligible to the unfamiliar listener. If by age three, your child's speech cannot be understood most of the time by others, a speech evaluation is recommended.

Articulating all the speech sounds correctly takes several years for most children to acquire. Up until seven years of age, some children may still have difficulty with /r/, /s/, and /th/ sounds as well as sound blends (words that have two or more consonant sounds together, such as /sl/, /str/, /thr/, etc.). Words that are lengthy and unfamiliar (for example, guacamole and escalator) will also take practice to produce correctly.

Conclusion

You may have noticed a common thread strung throughout all the activities in this book. This common thread is the approach that teaches, "More important than the activity itself is *how* we interact with our children." The scope of this approach is much larger than simply playing a game with a child. It is about fostering meaningful, trusted, open communication, which leads to successful relationships with children that will last well into their adulthood.

My hope is that through reading this book, a new thought process will evolve and become evidenced in your behaviors as you communicate with children. I think it is time we threw away old, hardened ways and treated each other, regardless of age, with respect as human beings. This challenge starts in babyhood, and does not end until the time of our deaths. We have a whole lifetime to establish and improve relationships, starting from the moment of birth. The compelling process of communication is our tool.

Sweet dreams.

Suggested Children's Books

The following books are recommended for children in the first three years of life. Many are boardbooks that will wipe clean with a damp cloth; others are small in size and easy for little hands to grasp; still others utilize bold colors and one or two pictures per page. All of these features are best suited to the small child's needs and level of understanding.

Sensory Books

Demi. *Fluffy bunny: A soft and furry boardbook.* New York: Grosset & Dunlap, 1987. Contains pictures of a fluffy bunny for baby to feel.
Demi. *Jolly koala bear: A soft and furry boardbook.* New York: Grosset & Dunlap, 1987. Contains pictures of a furry bear for baby to feel.
Demi. *Downy duckling: A soft and furry boardbook.* New York: Grosset & Dunlap, 1987. Contains pictures of a soft duck for baby to feel.
Harte, C. *My chalkboard book.* New York: Random House, 1988. A book with a built-in chalkboard and chalk; suitable to the two- and three-year-old.
Kline, S. *The hole book.* New York: Putnam, 1989. This book has holes for baby's busy, poking fingers.
Walley, D. *Crazy creatures.* Los Angeles: Price Stern Sloan, 1986.
Warne, F. *Mr. Jeremy Fisher: A Beatrice Potter bath book.* Ontario: Penguin

Books, Ltd., 1988. You can take this book into the bathtub; it's vinyl.
Pat the bunny, New York: Golden Press, 1988.
Little bunny follows his nose, New York: Golden Press, 1971.
Touch me book, New York: Golden Press, 1961. These books provide a variety of different textures for baby to feel.

Rhyme and Repetition

Blocksma, M. *Rub a dub dub, What's in the tub?* Chicago: Children's Press, 1984. Simple rhymes are repeated throughout the book.
Delacre, L. *Good time with baby.* New York: Grosset & Dunlap, 1989.
Fujikawa, G. *Baby Mother Goose.* New York: Grosset & Dunlap, 1989. Traditional Mother Goose stories.
Scarry, R. *Best Mother Goose ever.* New York: Golden Press, 1970. Mother Goose stories that are delightfully illustrated.
Suess, Dr. *The cat in the hat.* New York: Random House, 1957. The many Dr. Suess books available utilize rhyme and repetition that two- and three-year olds will ask for over and over again.
Suess, Dr. *Fox in sox.* New York: Random House, 1965.

Picture Books

Ahlberg, J., and Ahlberg, A. *The baby's catalogue.* Boston: Joy Street Books, 1982. Everything in a baby's life, from diaper pins to daddy.
Amery, H., and Cartwright, S. *The first hundred words.* Tulsa, OK: EDC Publishing, 1988. Vocabulary words for the Spanish-speaking child.
Oxenbury, H. *All fall down.* New York: Aladdin Books, 1987.
Oxenbury, H. *Clap hands.* New York: Aladdin Books, 1987.
Oxenbury, H. *Tickle, tickle.* New York: Aladdin Books, 1987.
Oxenbury, H. *Say goodnight.* New York: Aladdin Books, 1987. This se-

ries of board books is very simple and excellent for babies under one year of age.

Ricklen, N. *Mommy and me.* New York: Simon and Schuster, 1988.

The following Neil Ricklen books are recommended for the infant to one-year-old. The wipeable boardbooks feature colorful pictures of objects and people in baby's environment, with only one picture per page.

Daddy and me. New York: Simon and Schuster, 1988.

Baby's friends. New York: Simon and Schuster, 1986.

Baby's toys. New York: Simon and Schuster, 1986.

Baby's clothes. New York: Simon and Schuster, 1986.

Baby's home. New York: Simon and Schuster, 1986.

Salac, D. Christine. *Aleksandra, where is your nose?* New York: St. Martin's Press, 1986. Another simple boardbook for babies.

Silverman, M. *My little book of baby animals.* New York: Grosset & Dunlap, 1987.

Spier, P. *Gobble, growl, grunt: A book of animal sounds.* New York: Doubleday, 1988. The sounds leap right off the page in this cacophonous book of animal sounds!

Tyler, J. *Bedtime words.* Tulsa, OK: EDC Publishing, 1987.

Concept Books

Concept books illustrate the understanding of spatial location, opposites, categories, counting, color, shape recognition, and descriptive words. These are great for one- to three-year-olds.

Carter, D. A. *How many bugs in a box?* New York: Simon and Schuster, 1988.

Hoban, T. *Is it red? Is it yellow? Is it blue?* New York: Scholastic Books, 1978.

Hoban, T. *Push pull, empty full: A Book of Opposites.* New York: Macmillan, 1972.

Hoban, T. *Over, under and through and other spatial concepts.* New York: Macmillan, 1973.

Kunhardt, E. *Which one would you choose?* New York: Greenwillow, 1989.

Leslie, A. *Hidden animals.* New York: Dial, 1989.

Leslie, A. *Hidden toys.* New York: Dial, 1989.

Pragoff, F. *Shapes.* New York: Doubleday, 1989.

Spier, P. *Fast—slow, high—low.* New York: Doubleday, 1988.

Suggested Toys for Children
Birth–18 Months

As your child progresses from one stage of development to the next, he will play with the same toys in different ways. Many of the toys listed below are also suitable for children two years of age and older.

- Rattles
- Mobiles
- Mirror (placed at child's eye level)
- Busy boxes (with mirrors, sliding doors, a telephone dial, spinners, and buttons to push that squeak or make clicking sounds)
- Soft, furry, stuffed animals
- Dolls and accessories (doll clothes, hairbrush, bottle, toy cradle, blanket)
- Noisemakers (large ball with bells inside, music boxes, toys to shake with beads inside)
- Toy xylophone
- Pounding bench
- Large, cloth blocks
- Safe household containers for filling and emptying
- Small, wooden blocks for stacking

- Large and small balls
- Nesting cups, blocks, or cylinders
- Stacking rings
- Shape-sorting box with a top that opens
- Jack-in-the-Box
- Pop beads
- Bathtub toys
- Toy telephone
- Hand puppets
- Pull toys (those on wheels, pulled by a string)
- Push toys (play vacuum cleaner or lawn mower that makes clicking and clacking sounds; some even spew bubbles!)
- Washable boardbooks

Suggested Toys for Children

18 Months–3 Years

- Picture books
- Puzzles
- Shape sorter or shape ball (many different varieties)
- Large beads for stringing
- Peg boards
- Sewing cards
- Lotto games
- Musical recordings (folk, classical, and children's music)
- Balls of various sizes (beach, tennis, ping-pong)
- Bubbles, bubble pipes, soap suds
- Dolls and accessories (bottle, blanket, doll bed, tea set, clothes that zip, snap, and hook)
- Cars, trucks, airplanes, helicopters, and boats of various sizes (realistic or wooden replicas)
- Miniature toys that are easy to manipulate and can be hidden in and under things, or lined up in rows (little people, animals, road signs, vehicles)
- Building sets (Duplo blocks)
- Large and small blocks
- Dress-up clothes for boys as well as girls (shoes, hats, shirts, purses, beads, belts, bracelets)

- Household items for pretend play (keys, pots, and pans, dishes, play telephone, broom, kitchen utensils, blankets, boxes, plastic food items or real cans of food, etc.)
- Art materials like washable paints and markers, white paper and construction paper, blunt-nose scissors, white glue, and crayons
- Playscapes (commercial wooden train and track set, dollhouse, farm, gas station—can use miniature toys with playscapes)
- Containers for carrying things, such as old wallets, grocery bags, lunch boxes, Tupperware, suitcases, briefcases
- For outdoor play, push-and-pull cars and wagons, tricycles, small slide and jungle gym, swings, large cardboard appliance boxes
- Sandbox and large tubs for outdoor water play (scoops, spoons, sticks, containers, sponges, cups, sieves, sifters)
- Rocking horse with springs

Bibliography

Bates, L. A., and F. Illg. *Your two year old: Terrible or tender?* New York: Dell Publishing Co., 1976.

Beck, M. S. *Baby talk—How your child learns to speak.* New York: New American Library, 1979.

Bolles, E. B. *So much to say: How to help your child learn to talk.* New York: St. Martin's Press, 1982.

Bower, T. G. R. *A primer of infant development.* San Francisco: W. H. Freeman and Co., 1977.

Brazelton, T. B., Koslowski, B., and Main, M. The Origins of Reciprocity: The Early Mother–Infant Interaction. In M. Lewis and L. Rosenblum (Eds.), *Origins of behaviors, Vol. 1.* New York: Wiley, 1974.

Caplan, F. *The first twelve months of life.* New York: Bantam Books, 1988.

Caplan, F. *The second twelve months of life.* New York: Bantam Books, 1985.

Cutting, B. *Talk your way to reading (Helping your child with language).* Auckland, New Zealand: Shortland Publications, 1985.

Dunst, Carl J. *Infant learning. A cognitive-linguistic intervention strategy.* Hingham, MA: Teaching Resources, 1985.

Faber, A., and E. Mazlish. *Siblings without rivalry.* New York: W. W. Norton & Co., 1987.

Hatten, J. T., and P. W. Hatten. *Natural language.* Tucson, AZ: Communication Skill Builders, 1975.

Holt, J. *How children learn.* New York: Dell Publishing Co., 1983.

Honig, A. S. Tuning in to toddlers: A communication challenge. *Early Child Development and Care*, 25:207–219, 1986.

Landreth, C. *Preschool learning and teaching.* New York: Harper & Row, 1972.

Lehane, S. *Help your baby learn: 100 Piaget-based activities for the first two years of life.* Englewood Cliffs, NJ: Prentice-Hall, 1976.

McClowry, D. P., A. M. Guilford, and S. O. Richardson. *Infant communication: Development, assessment, and intervention.* Philadelphia, PA: Grune & Stratton, 1982.

Manolson, A. *It takes two to talk.* Toronto, Ontario: Hanen Early Language Resource Centre, 1983.

Marshall, H. K., and M. O. Robertson. *Birth, interaction and attachment.* New Brunswick, NJ: Johnson & Johnson Baby Products Company, 1982.

Menlove, C. K. *Ready, set, go!* Englewood Cliffs, NJ: Prentice-Hall, 1978.

Rubin, R. R., and J. J. Fisher. *Your preschooler.* New York: Macmillan, 1982.

Schreiber, F. R. *Your child's speech.* New York: Random House, 1973.

Index

Age level
  activity selection and, 4
  babbling stage (4-6 months), 23-38
  "baby talk," advice on use of,
    237-238
  control talk stage (22-24 months),
    137-155
  conversation stage (31-33 months),
    197-216
  expanded learning stage (28-30
    months), 179-195
  first-word stage (10-12 months),
    57-76
  jargon talk stage (13-15 months),
    77-98
  language delay problem, 244-245
  listening stage (25-27 months),
    157-177
  motor development stage (7-9
    months), 39-56
  newborn (birth-3 months), 7-22
  problem-solving stage (34-36
    months), 217-236
  understanding stage (16-18
    months), 99-118
  vocabulary growth stage (19-21
    months), 119-135

All gone activity, understanding
    stage (16-18 months), 110
Animal placemats, problem-solving
    stage (34-36 months), 234-235
Animal talk activity, jargon talk stage
    (13-15 months), 84-85
Animal walk activity, conversation
    stage (31-33 months), 201-202
Art
  crayon doodle, listening stage
    (25-27 months), 162-164
  finger painting, expanded learning
    stage (28-30 months), 184-185
  hand print activity, expanded
    learning stage (28-30 months),
    187-188
  sandpaper circles activity, problem-
    solving stage (34-36 months),
    226-227
  scribble art activity, understanding
    stage (16-18 months), 110-112
Articulation. *See* Pronunciation
Attention-getting behavior, babbling
    stage (4-6 months), 29-30

Babbling, motor development stage
    (7-9 months), 39-40

263

Babbling stage (4-6 months), 23-38
  abilities in, 23-24
  daily activities, 34-37
  developmental milestones, 24-25
  playtime activities, 25-34
  stimulation techniques, 37-38
"Baby talk," advice on use of,
    237-238. *See also* Motherese
Balance, walk the plank activity, con-
    versation stage (31-33 months),
    206-207
Balloon play
  sail the balloon activity, conversa-
    tion stage (31-33 months),
    207-208
  understanding stage (16-18
    months), 105-106
Balls
  ball roll activity, jargon talk stage
    (13-15 months), 89-90
  bowling activity, control talk stage
    (22-24 months), 146-147
  kick ball activity, vocabulary
    growth stage (19-21 months),
    125-126
  Ping-Pong ball activity, control talk
    stage (22-24 months), 144
Band leader activity, control talk
    stage (22-24 months), 146
Bathing
  babbling stage (4-6 months), 36-37
  body parts activity, expanded
    learning stage (28-30 months),
    192-193
  control talk stage (22-24 months),
    152-153
  empty and full activity, vocabulary
    growth stage (19-21 months),
    134
  first-word stage (10-12 months), 73
  hand washing activity, vocabulary
    growth stage (19-21 months),
    133-134

Bathing (*cont.*)
  jargon talk stage (13-15 months),
    94-95
  motorboat fun activity, listening
    stage (25-27 months), 174
  motor development stage (7-9
    months), 53-54
  newborn (birth-3 months), 20
  people toy play activity, conversa-
    tion stage (31-33 months),
    212-213
  swimming activity, problem-
    solving stage (34-36 months),
    234
  understanding stage (16-18
    months), 115-116
Bedtime activity, understanding stage
    (16-18 months), 116-117
Bellybutton activity, expanded learn-
    ing stage (28-30 months),
    192-193
Bicycle kicks, babbling stage (4-6
    months), 33
Bilingualism, advice on, 239-240
Birth order, language skills and, 239,
    240
Blocks
  block banging activity, motor de-
    velopment stage (7-9 months),
    49-50
  building block activity, control talk
    stage (22-24 months), 141-142
Body activity, listening stage (25-27
    months), 165-166. *See also* Mo-
    tor skills; Motor development
    stage
Body language, first-word stage
    (10-12 months), 75. *See also*
    Facial expression
Body parts learning
  first-word stage (10-12 months), 73
  motor development stage (7-9
    months), 53-54

Body rub. *See* Massage

Books. *See* Reading

Bouncing activity
babbling stage (4-6 months), 34
first-word stage (10-12 months),
69-70

Bowling activity, control talk stage
(22-24 months), 146-147

Box activity, vocabulary growth stage
(19-21 months), 128-129

Brain teaser activity, problem-solving
stage (34-36 months), 229

Brand new words activity, conversation stage (31-33 months),
202

Brush my teeth activity, conversation
stage (31-33 months), 213

Bubble chase activity, listening stage
(25-27 months), 164-165

Bubble pan activity, control talk stage
(22-24 months), 142-144

Building block activity, control talk
stage (22-24 months), 141-
142

Car and truck activity, vocabulary
growth stage (19-21 months),
127-128

Cave activity, expanded learning
stage (28-30 months), 189-191

Chase me activity, vocabulary growth
stage (19-21 months), 130

Choice
clothing
problem-solving stage (34-36
months), 231-232
understanding stage (16-18
months), 113-114, 115
foods, motor development stage
(7-9 months), 53

Cleaning, control talk stage (22-24
months), 153

Clothes. *See also* Dressing
clothes sorting activity, expanded
learning stage (28-30 months),
191
dressing, problem-solving stage
(34-36 months), 231-232

Cold and hot recognition, jargon talk
stage (13-15 months), 94-95

Collections, rock collection, expanded learning stage (28-30
months), 185-186

Color naming activity, listening stage
(25-27 months), 172

Commands
string ring activity, conversation
stage (31-33 months), 208-209
understanding stage (16-18
months), 99-100

Communication
babbling stage (4-6 months), 37-38
conversation stage (31-33 months),
stimulation techniques,
213-216
first-word stage (10-12 months), 75
listening and, 117-118
listening stage (25-27 months),
176-177
motor development stage (7-9
months), 40
rubbing noses activity, listening
stage (25-27 months), 169-171

Communication system
language and, 1-2
play and, 3-4

Container play, jargon talk stage
(13-15 months), 85-87

Control talk stage (22-24 months),
137-155
daily activities, 150-153
developmental milestones, 139-140
overview of, 137-138
playtime activities, 140-150
stimulation techniques, 153-155

Conversation, listening stage (25-27 months), 176-177
Conversation stage (31-33 months), 197-216
  daily activities, 211-213
  developmental milestones, 198-200
  overview of, 197-198
  playtime activities, 200-211
  stimulation techniques, 213-216
Cooing
  newborn (birth-3 months), 8
  vocal play, newborn (birth-3 months), 12-13
Cooking activity, expanded learning stage (28-30 months), 191-192
Copycat activity
  first-word stage (10-12 months), 62-63, 67
  jargon talk stage (13-15 months), 77
  motor development stage (7-9 months), 45-46
Counting activity, understanding stage (16-18 months), 108-110
Crayon doodle, listening stage (25-27 months), 162-164
Crying
  communication system and, 1-2
  newborn (birth-3 months), 8, 17
Cuddling activity
  babbling stage (4-6 months), 27
  newborn (birth-3 months), 10-11
Cup drinking
  first-word stage (10-12 months), 72-73
  motor development stage (7-9 months), 54-55
Cutting activity, problem-solving stage (34-36 months), 232-233

Daily activities
  babbling stage (4-6 months), 34-37

Daily activities (*cont.*)
  control talk stage (22-24 months), 150-153
  conversation stage (31-33 months), 211-213
  first-word stage (10-12 months), 71-75
  jargon talk stage (13-15 months), 93-95
  listening stage (25-27 months), 172-176
  motor development stage (7-9 months), 52-55
  newborn (birth-3 months), 18-22
  problem-solving stage (34-36 months), 231-235
  understanding stage (16-18 months), 113-117
  vocabulary growth stage (19-21 months), 131-134
Dance, scarf dance activity, conversation stage (31-33 months), 204-205
Dance and prance activity, newborn (birth-3 months), 17
Day care facility, understanding stage (16-18 months), 117
Dental care, conversation stage (31-33 months), 213
Developmental milestones
  babbling stage (4-6 months), 24-25
  control talk stage (22-24 months), 139-140
  conversation stage (31-33 months), 198-200
  expanded learning stage (28-30 months), 180-182
  first-word stage (10-12 months), 59-61
  jargon talk stage (13-15 months), 79-80
  listening stage (25-27 months), 158-160

Developmental milestones (*cont.*)
motor development stage (7-9 months), 41-43
newborn (birth-3 months), 9-10
problem-solving stage (34-36 months), 218-220
understanding stage (16-18 months), 101-102
vocabulary growth stage (19-21 months), 120-122
Diapering, first-word stage (10-12 months), 71-72
Directions. *See* Commands
Discipline, control talk stage (22-24 months), 137-155. *See also* Control talk stage
Disfluent speech, problem spotting, 246-248
Doll play activity
control talk stage (22-24 months), 148-150
paper doll cutouts, problem-solving stage (34-36 months), 148-150
Dressing
autonomy in, conversation stage (31-33 months), 211
clothes sorting activity, expanded learning stage (28-30 months), 191
color naming activity, listening stage (25-27 months), 172
control talk stage (22-24 months), 150
first-word stage (10-12 months), 71-72
jargon talk stage (13-15 months), 93
motor development stage (7-9 months), 52-53
undressing skills, listening stage (25-27 months), 174-176

Dressing (*cont.*)
vocabulary growth stage (19-21 months), 131
zip my coat activity, expanded learning stage (28-30 months), 193

Empty and full activity, vocabulary growth stage (19-21 months), 134
Exercise activity, expanded learning stage (28-30 months), 186-187
Expanded learning stage (28-30 months), 179-195
daily activities, 191-193
developmental milestones, 180-182
overview of, 179-180
playtime activities, 182-192
stimulation techniques, 193-195
Eye contact
listening skills, 157-158
stimulation techniques, newborn (birth-3 months), 22
vocal play, newborn (birth-3 months), 12-13
Eye-hand coordination, babbling stage (4-6 months), 34
Eye movements
babbling stage (4-6 months), 34-35
infancy, 20-21

Face recognition
first-word stage (10-12 months), 66
newborn (birth-3 months), 15-16
Facial expression
babbling stage (4-6 months), 29
listening skills, 158
newborn (birth-3 months), 13
smile elicitation, babbling stage (4-6 months), 32-33
understanding stage (16-18 months), 99

Fathering, importance of, 238
Feeding
  all gone activity, 110
  babbling stage (4-6 months), 37
  choice activity, understanding
    stage (16-18 months), 115
  control talk stage (22-24 months),
    151-152, 153
  cutting/slicing/peeling activity,
    232-233
  first-word stage (10-12 months),
    72-75
  jargon talk stage (13-15 months),
    93-94, 95
  newborn (birth-3 months), 17
  sandwich making activity,
    problem-solving stage (34-36
    months), 233-234
  spoons and forks activity, 172-173
  table setting activity, conversation
    stage (31-33 months), 211-212
  vocabulary growth stage (19-21
    months), 131-132
Feely grab bag activity, listening
  stage (25-27 months), 166-168
Finger painting, expanded learning
  stage (28-30 months), 184-185
Finger play
  babbling period (4-6 months), 27
  jargon talk stage (13-15 months),
    80-82
Firstborn, language skills and, 239,
  240
First-word stage (10-12 months),
  57-76
  abilities in, 57-59
  daily activities, 71-75
  developmental milestones, 59-61
  playtime activities, 61-71
  stimulation techniques, 75-76
Flour play activity, vocabulary
  growth stage (19-21 months),
  122-123

Fly with wings activity, listening
  stage (25-27 months), 165-166
Follow the ring activity, newborn
  (birth-3 months), 20-21
Forks and spoons activity, listening
  stage (25-27 months), 172-173
Fork use, control talk stage (22-24
  months), 151-152
Future/past construction, control talk
  stage (22-24 months), 154-155

Grammar. *See* Sentence construction
Grasping activity
  babbling stage (4-6 months), 25-26
  jargon talk stage (13-15 months),
    85-87
  motor development stage (7-9
    months), 46-47
  newborn (birth-3 months), 16
Greeting behavior activity, motor development stage (7-9 months),
  50-51
Grocery shopping, expanded learning stage (28-30 months),
  183-184

Hand print activity, expanded learning stage (28-30 months),
  187-188
Hand washing activity, vocabulary
  growth stage (19-21 months),
  133-134
Happy and sad activity, listening
  stage (25-27 months), 171-172
Hats on activity, first-word stage
  (10-12 months), 62-63
Hearing ability
  assessment of, 36
  babbling stage (4-6 months), 29
  problem spotting, 245-246
Heavy and light activity, expanded
  learning stage (28-30 months),
  188-189

"Hi" and "bye-bye" activity, motor
    development stage (7-9
    months), 50-51
Hide-and-seek, jargon talk stage
    (13-15 months), 87-88
Horsey ride activity, first-word stage
    (10-12 months), 69-70
Hot and cold recognition, jargon talk
    stage (13-15 months), 94-95
Humor
    acquisition by child, 97
    importance of, 4-5

"I Forgot" activity, control talk stage
    (22-24 months), 140-141
Imagination. See also Pretend play
    cave activity, expanded learning
        stage (28-30 months), 189-191
    pantomime time activity, conversa-
        tion stage (31-33 months),
        203-204
    puppet show activity, expanded
        learning stage (28-30 months),
        182-183
Imitation. See Copycat activity
Individual differences, motor devel-
    opment stage (7-9 months), 43
Infancy. See also Age level
    babbling stage (4-6 months), 23-38
    motor development stage (7-9
        months), 39-56
    newborn (birth-3 months), 7-22
Infant mobiles, newborn (birth-3
    months), 14
Intelligence quotient, speech and,
    239
Interpersonal relationships
    babbling stage (4-6 months), 27-29
    communication system and, 1-2
    language acquisition and, 4
    motor development stage (7-9
        months), 40, 46, 50-51
    newborn (birth-3 months), 13

Interpersonal relationships (cont.)
    thank you activity, understanding
        stage (16-18 months), 112
"I want that" activity, motor develop-
    ment stage (7-9 months), 46-47

Jargon talk stage (13-15 months),
    77-98
    abilities in, 77-79
    daily activities, 93-95
    developmental milestones, 79-80
    playtime activities, 80-93
    stimulation techniques, 95-98
Jumping bean activity, listening stage
    (25-27 months), 168

Kick ball activity, vocabulary growth
    stage (19-21 months), 125-126

Labeling
    control talk stage (22-24 months),
        148
    parts of a whole activity, problem-
        solving stage (34-36 months),
        224-225
    reading ability and, 104
    vocabulary growth stage (19-21
        months), 119
    "What's it for?" activity, conversa-
        tion stage (31-33 months),
        209-211
Ladder walk activity, control talk
    stage (22-24 months), 144-145
Language, communication system
    and, 1-2
Language acquisition. See also Speech
    developmental stages in, 100
    first word, 58-59
    interpersonal relationships and, 4
    jargon talk stage (13-15 months),
        97
    motor development stage (7-9
        months), 40, 43

Language acquisition (*cont.*)
  problem spotting, 243-249
  sex differences, 240-241
Laundry, expanded learning stage
    (28-30 months), 191
Listening, understanding stage (16-18
    months), 117-118
Listening stage (25-27 months),
    157-177
  daily activities, 172-176
  developmental milestones, 158-160
  overview of, 157-158
  playtime activities, 160-172
  stimulation techniques, 176-177
Low birthweight infants, cuddling
    activities and, 10

Massage
  babbling stage (4-6 months), 31-32
  newborn (birth-3 months), 18-19
Megaphone activity, vocabulary
    growth stage (19-21 months),
    124-125
Mirroring, jargon talk stage (13-15
    months), 77
Mirror play
  babbling stage (4-6 months), 30-31
  motor development stage (7-9
    months), 41
Mispronunciation, corrections of,
    134-135
Mobiles, newborn (birth-3 months),
    14
Mood, happy and sad activity, listen-
    ing stage (25-27 months),
    171-172
Motherese, stimulation by, 23-24. *See
    also* "Baby talk"
Motorboat fun activity, listening
    stage (25-27 months), 174
Motor development stage (7-9
    months), 39-56
  abilities in, 39-41

Motor development stage (*cont.*)
  daily activities, 52-55
  developmental milestones, 41-43
  playtime activities, 43-52
  stimulation techniques, 55-56
Motor skills
  animal walk activity, conversation
    stage (31-33 months), 201-202
  babbling stage (4-6 months), 25,
    33-34
  control talk stage (22-24 months),
    139, 144-145
  conversation stage (31-33 months),
    199
  exercise activity, expanded learning
    stage (28-30 months), 186-187
  expanded learning stage (28-30
    months), 181
  first-word stage (10-12 months), 60,
    64, 68
  heavy and light activity, expanded
    learning stage (28-30 months),
    188-189
  jargon talk stage (13-15 months),
    79-80
  jumping bean activity, listening
    stage (25-27 months), 168
  listening stage (25-27 months), 159,
    165-166
  motor development stage (7-9
    months), 42
  newborn (birth-3 months), 9
  obstacle course activity, conversa-
    tion stage (31-33 months),
    200-201
  problem-solving stage (34-36
    months), 219
  running, problem-solving stage
    (34-36 months), 230-231
  scarf dance activity, conversation
    stage (31-33 months), 204-205
  speech production and, 78
  spoon use, 95

Motor skills (*cont.*)
  understanding stage (16-18
    months), 101
  vocabulary growth stage (19-21
    months), 121, 129-130
  walk the plank activity, conversa-
    tion stage (31-33 months),
    206-207
Moving objects, newborn (birth-3
  months), 20-21
Music
  band leader activity, control talk
    stage (22-24 months), 146
  piano player activity, understand-
    ing stage (16-18 months),
    106-107
  scarf dance activity, conversation
    stage (31-33 months), 204-205
  song
    counting activity and, 109
    first-word stage (10-12 months),
      70-71, 73
    jargon talk stage (13-15 months),
      80-81
    motor development stage (7-9
      months), 50
    Ring around the Rosey activity,
      126

Name recognition
  animal talk activity, 84-85
  listening stage (25-27 months), 157
  motor development stage (7-9
    months), 41, 48
Name response
  jargon talk stage (13-15 months),
    92
  newborn (birth-3 months), 13
Naming. *See* Labeling
Neonate. *See* Newborn
Newborn (birth-3 months), 7-22. *See*
  also Age level; Infancy
  abilities of, 7

Newborn (*cont.*)
  daily activities, 18-21
  developmental milestones of, 9-10
  expressive communication of, 8
  motor skills of, 9
  playtime activities in, 10-18
  stimulation techniques, 22
  toy play of, 9-10
No. *See* Control talk stage
Noise activity. *See* Sounds activity

Obstacle course activity, conversation
  stage (31-33 months), 200-201
Old McDonald song activity, motor
  development stage (7-9
  months), 50
Onomatopoeie, first-word stage
  (10-12 months), 75-76
Outdoor activities
  control talk stage (22-24 months),
    150
  problem-solving stage (34-36
    months), 221-223
  running, problem-solving stage
    (34-36 months), 230-231
  textures, 126-127

Pantomime time activity, conversation stage (31-33 months),
  203-204
Pants on activity, babbling stage (4-6
  months), 34-35
Paper doll cutouts, problem-solving
  stage (34-36 months), 231-232
Paper megaphone activity, vocabulary growth stage (19-21
  months), 124-125
Parts of a whole activity, problem-
  solving stage (34-36 months),
  224-225
Past/future construction, control talk
  stage (22-24 months), 154-155

Patty cake activity
    first-word stage (10-12 months),
        67-68
    motor development stage (7-9
        months), 45-46
Peeling activity, problem-solving
    stage (34-36 months), 232-233
People toy play activity, conversation
    stage (31-33 months), 212-213
Photographs, scrap book activity, un-
    derstanding stage (16-18
    months), 103-104
Piano player activity, understanding
    stage (16-18 months), 106-107
Ping-Pong ball activity, control talk
    stage (22-24 months), 144
Placemats, animal placemats,
    problem-solving stage (34-36
    months), 234-235
Plant watering activity, problem-
    solving stage (34-36 months),
    227-228
Playtime activities
    communication system and, 3-4
    control talk stage (22-24 months),
        140-150
    conversation stage (31-33 months),
        200-211
    expanded learning stage (28-30
        months), 182-192
    first-word stage (10-12 months),
        61-71
    jargon talk stage (13-15 months),
        80-93
    motor development stage (7-9
        months), 43-52
    newborn (birth-3 months), 10-18
    problem-solving stage (34-36
        months), 220-231
    time scheduling, babbling stage
        (4-6 months), 38
    understanding stage (16-18
        months), 102-112

Playtime activities (cont.)
    vocabulary growth stage (19-21
        months), 122-131
Plurals, expanded learning stage
    (28-30 months), 195
Poetry reading, listening stage (25-27
    months), 160-161
Pointing, motor development stage
    (7-9 months), 53
Prance and dance activity, newborn
    (birth-3 months), 17
Premature infants
    cuddling activities and, 10
    problem spotting, 245
Pretend play. See also Imagination
    building block activity, 142
    cave activity, expanded learning
        stage (28-30 months), 189-191
    vocabulary growth stage (19-21
        months), 131-132
Problem-solving skills, vocabulary
    growth stage (19-21 months),
    128-129
Problem-solving stage (34-36
    months), 217-236
    daily activities, 231-235
    developmental milestones, 218-220
    overview of, 217-218
    playtime activities, 220-231
    stimulation techniques, 235-236
Problem spotting, 243-249
    disfluent speech, 246-248
    hearing problems, 245-246
    language delay, 244-245
    overview of, 243-244
    voice problems, 248-249
Pronunciation
    articulation, voice problem spot-
        ting, 249
    corrections of, 134-135
Puppet show activity, expanded
    learning stage (28-30 months),
    182-183

Purse play activity, understanding
    stage (16-18 months), 107-108
Puzzle play, problem-solving stage
    (34-36 months), 225-226

Raisin bottle activity, vocabulary
    growth stage (19-21 months),
    129-130
Rattles
    babbling stage (4-6 months), 25-26
    wrist rattles, newborn (birth-3
        months), 11-12
Reading
    first-word stage (10-12 months),
        61-62
    listening stage (25-27 months),
        160-161
    problem-solving stage (34-36
        months), 223-224
    rhyme time activity, problem-
        solving stage (34-36 months),
        229-230
    scrap book activity, understanding
        stage (16-18 months), 104
    suggested book list, 253-256
Rhyme time activity, problem-solving
    stage (34-36 months), 229-230
Ring around the Rosey activity, vo-
    cabulary growth stage (19- 21
    months), 126
Rock collection, expanded learning
    stage (28-30 months), 185-186
Rubbing noses activity, listening
    stage (25-27 months), 169-171

Sail the balloon activity, conversation
    stage (31-33 months), 207-208
Sandpaper circles activity, problem-
    solving stage (34-36 months),
    226-227
Sandwich making activity, problem-
    solving stage (34-36 months),
    233-234

Saying "no." See Control talk stage
Scarf dance activity, conversation
    stage (31-33 months), 204-205
Scheduling, play time, babbling stage
    (4-6 months), 38
Scrap book activity
    problem-solving stage (34-36
        months), 223-224
    understanding stage (16-18
        months), 103-104
Scribble art activity, understanding
    stage (16-18 months), 110-112
Sense of humor. See Humor
Senses
    feely grab bag activity, 166-168
    outdoor activities, textures, 126-127
    rubbing noses activity, listening
        stage (25-27 months), 169-171
    sandpaper circles activity, problem-
        solving stage (34-36 months),
        226-227
    touch and texture, newborn
        (birth-3 months), 14
Sentence construction
    control talk stage (22-24 months),
        154
    expanded learning stage (28-30
        months), 194-195
    rhyme time activity, problem-
        solving stage (34-36 months),
        229-230
Separation
    babbling stage (4-6 months), 27
    first-word stage (10-12 months),
        66
    motor development stage (7-9
        months), 44-45
Sex differences, language acquisition
    and, 240-241
Shadow talk activity, expanded learn-
    ing stage (28-30 months), 183
Shoe activity, understanding stage
    (16-18 months), 113-114

Siblings, motor development stage (7-9 months), 41

Sing a bath song activity, babbling stage (4-6 months), 36-37

Skin contact. *See* Cuddling activity

Sleep activity, understanding stage (16-18 months), 116-117

Slicing activity, problem-solving stage (34-36 months), 232-233

Smelling flowers, jargon talk stage (13-15 months), 92-93

Smile elicitation, babbling stage (4-6 months), 32-33

Snowman, expanded learning stage (28-30 months), 188

Social behavior. *See* Interpersonal relationships

Socialization, motor development stage (7-9 months), 40-41

Song. *See also* Music
counting activity and, 109
first-word stage (10-12 months), 70-71, 73
jargon talk stage (13-15 months), 80-81
motor development stage (7-9 months), 50
Ring around the Rosey activity, 126

Sounds activity
babbling stage (4-6 months), 35-36
jargon talk stage (13-15 months), 82-83
listening stage (25-27 months), 162
motor development stage (7-9 months), 49-50

Speech
control talk stage (22-24 months), 139
conversation stage (31-33 months), 198-199
disfluent speech, problem spotting, 246-248
expanded learning stage (28-30 months), 180-181

Speech (*cont.*)
first-word stage (10-12 months), 59-60
intelligence quotient and, 239
jargon talk stage (13-15 months), 79
listening stage (25-27 months), 158-159
motor development stage (7-9 months), 41-42, 43
problem-solving stage (34-36 months), 218-219
understanding stage (16-18 months), 101
vocabulary growth stage (19-21 months), 120-121

Spoons and forks activity, listening stage (25-27 months), 172-173

Spoon use, jargon talk stage (13-15 months), 95

Stair climbing activity, first-word stage (10-12 months), 68

Stimulation techniques
babbling stage (4-6 months), 23-24, 37-38
control talk stage (22-24 months), 153-155
conversation stage (31-33 months), 213-216
expanded learning stage (28-30 months), 193-195
first-word stage (10-12 months), 75-76
jargon talk stage (13-15 months), 95-98
listening stage (25-27 months), 176-177
motor development stage (7-9 months), 55-56
newborn (birth-3 months), 22
problem-solving stage (34-36 months), 235-236
understanding stage (16-18 months), 117-118

Stimulation techniques (*cont.*)
   vocabulary growth stage (19-21
      months), 134-135
Storm watcher activity, conversation
   stage (31-33 months), 205-206
Story ability, listening stage (25-27
   months), 157
String pull activity, jargon talk stage
   (13-15 months), 88-89
String ring activity, conversation
   stage (31-33 months), 208-209
Stuttering, disfluent speech, problem
   spotting, 246-248
Swimming activity, problem-solving
   stage (34-36 months), 234

Table setting activity, conversation
   stage (31-33 months), 211-212
Talking. *See* Speech
Tape recorder activity, problem-
   solving stage (34-36 months),
   220-221
Telephone talk activity, understanding stage (16-18 months),
   102-103
"Thank you" activity, understanding
   stage (16-18 months), 112
Toe and finger play, babbling stage
   (4-6 months), 27
Tooth brushing activity, conversation
   stage (31-33 months), 213
Touch. *See* Cuddling activity;
   Massage
Touch and texture. *See* Senses
Toy play
   babbling stage (4-6 months), 25, 33
   control talk stage (22-24 months),
      139-140
   conversation stage (31-33 months),
      199-200
   expanded learning stage (28-30
      months), 181-182
   first-word stage (10-12 months),
      60-61

Toy play (*cont.*)
   jargon talk stage (13-15 months),
      80, 83-84
   listening stage (25-27 months),
      159-160
   motor development stage (7-9
      months), 42-43, 56
   newborn (birth-3 months), 9-10
   problem-solving stage (34-36
      months), 219-220
   understanding stage (16-18
      months), 102
   vocabulary growth stage (19-21
      months), 121-122
Toys, suggested toy list, 257-260
Toy wrap activity, jargon talk stage
   (13-15 months), 90-92
Train activity, vocabulary growth
   stage (19-21 months), 123-124
Tumble time activity, understanding
   stage (16-18 months), 104-105
Turn taking
   babbling stage (4-6 months), 27-29
   communication, 55

Understanding
   control talk stage (22-24 months),
      139
   conversation stage (31-33 months),
      198-199
   expanded learning stage (28-30
      months), 180-181
   first-word stage (10-12 months),
      59-60
   jargon talk stage (13-15 months),
      79
   listening stage (25-27 months),
      158-159
   motor development stage (7-9
      months), 41-42
   problem-solving stage (34-36
      months), 218-219
   vocabulary growth stage (19-21
      months), 120-121

Understanding stage (16-18 months),
99-118
abilities in, 99-100
daily activities, 113-117
developmental milestones, 101-102
playtime activities, 102-112
stimulation techniques, 117-118
Undressing skills, listening stage
(25-27 months), 174-176
Up we go activity, babbling stage (4-6
months), 33-34

Vocabulary
brand new words activity, conversation stage (31-33 months),
202
expanded learning stage (28-30
months), 179
understanding stage (16-18
months), 100
Vocabulary growth stage (19-21
months), 119-135
abilities of, 119-120
daily activities, 131-134
developmental milestones, 120-122
playtime activities, 122-131
stimulation techniques, 134-135
Vocal play
babbling stage (4-6 months), 23
newborn (birth-3 months), 12-13
Voice problems, problem spotting,
248-249

Walk the plank activity, conversation
stage (31-33 months), 206-207
Water, newborn (birth-3 months),
19-20. *See also* Bathing
Watering plants activity, problem-
solving stage (34-36 months),
227-228
Weather, storm watcher activity, conversation stage (31-33 months),
205-206
"What's it for?" activity, conversation
stage (31-33 months), 209-211
"Where did baby go?" activity, motor
development stage (7-9
months), 43-45
Whispering activity, listening stage
(25-27 months), 161-162
Willfullness
control talk stage (22-24 months),
138
vocabulary growth stage (19-21
months), 120
Window watch activity, control talk
stage (22-24 months), 148
Word recognition, animal talk activity, 84-85
Wrist rattles, newborn (birth-3
months), 11-12

"Zip my coat" activity, expanded
learning stage (28-30 months),
193